Mondrian's Map

RON HAUGE

• DENVER

PUBLISHER'S LETTER
BY MICHAEL GERBER

Beautiful Bums

As a drunk man once shouted at me, "Jobs are for knobs!"

Whenever a young person asks me how to get a job, my answer is always the same: "Don't."

"But how will I eat?"

"I've always managed somehow, you can too." Then I pay for lunch.

The kids think I'm crazy and maybe I am. All I can say is, my periods of sincere, bone-deep misery have come working for someone else. Conversely, my greatest professional happiness has been doing this, and *Bystander* has the same relation to A JOB as a muppet does to a real monster.

Jobs suck. This isn't debatable; if they didn't, they wouldn't have to threaten you with homelessness just to make you show up. Being OK with this state of affairs isn't growing up. It's how our society *keeps* from growing up. The post-COVID staff crunch gives me hope.

My first adult job set the tone; it was boring, underpaid, and illegal. I worked for a newsletter publisher who paid me to read medical articles and write extracts. He would then sell these to doctors too cheap to buy *JAMA*, *The Lancet*, etc. The beauty part, from my boss's perspective, was when the publishers got wind of this larceny (as they inevitably would) he could point his finger at me and say, "That independent contractor sold it to me! Sue him!"

This moldy baloney sandwich of a man strutted around, thinking he'd really figured something out, when all he'd really done was take advantage of my need to eat. At 22, I would've been happy to be mostly ghost, only material enough to move a pen or turn the pages of *The Benchley Roundup*. Being corporeal, I was fucked. After a few months, I noticed I was spending a lot of time at The Anchor Bar across the street; rather than become an alcoholic, I quit.

"Do you have another job?"

"No," I said. (I never did.)

"Bum." Baloney Sandwich smiled coldly, like he had beaten me somehow. But I'd showed who owned me, and it wasn't him.

"Maybe," I said, "but I'm beautiful."

That story, in various guises, was my entire 20s. I met a lot of nice people, people I liked, people doing the best they could. Everybody needs to eat. But whether I was in some dingy office in Long Island City, or Floor 7 of 30 Rock, sooner or later they'd ask me to do something stupid, shitty or illegal and I'd turn back into that beautiful bum. With every departure, I became more determined to work for myself—if I was going to have to do something stupid, shitty or illegal, I wanted to do it for *me*.

I temped a lot. This allowed me to take meetings with various members of the horsey set, asking if they'd like to fund a humor magazine. None did, but a few *almost* did, and I think of them and their tea cakes with great fondness. The Nineties were a kinder time, when the rich and bored would fund the occasional publication without insisting it advocate the use of poor children as firewood.

I worked at financial firms downtown, most of whom offered me permanent jobs. Over and over, I turned them down, to give my dreams more time to materialize. Meanwhile, college friends who'd donned comfortable yokes six or seven years before were starting to do interesting things; and it was becoming clear that, while my ideas were getting more and more marketable, the glint of promise conferred by a fancy college had gone. I was now just another broke asshole with good ideas, the kind of guy you'd either steal from or ignore. Showbiz runs on these people, but they never cash in; they can't, if all the money's going to stay at the top. So I met a girl from Chicago, fell in love, and left behind every contact I had in publishing and comedy. It was career suicide.

It also saved my life. Three months later on the morning of September 11, I stood in the front room of our weird, unheated flat in Chicago, watching the place I used to work collapse. I still can't watch that footage; if I'd stayed in New York, I would've probably been temping at Shearson/American Express in Tower One. And I would've gone back into the building after that first all clear, before the second plane. Because, y'know, I needed to eat.

Looking back, I feel two things: grateful amazement at how everything worked out, and how much the young me wanted a job. Jobs are what adults do; to be unemployed is to stay a kid. I desperately wanted to work someplace with cool people doing something not-awful that benefited all of us and, ideally, the world. It never happened, but I never stopped trying. The year before I started working on *Bystander*, I answered an ad to be a copywriter at a hip greeting card company. My cover letter is at right. (I didn't get the job.)

Now, thanks to all of you beautiful bums, I'm gainfully employed. I hope *Bystander* lasts forever, but whenever I think it might not, I hear that 22-year-old: "But how will I eat?"

To quote one of History's most beautiful bums, "Consider the lilies of the field." Certain lucky people seem to be able to live on love; *The Bystander* allows me to do just that. Merry Christmas to all the lilies of the field, and to the rest of you beautiful bums as well. **B**

MICHAEL GERBER (@mgerber937) is Editor & Publisher of *The American Bystander*.

BY 2011, I WAS SO BORED with cover letters. No interview, but I did hear from a editor. "Who ARE you?" Soon after, Brian and Alan rang. "Have you ever heard of Brian's magazine, *The American Bystander*?"

SHOULD I APPLY FOR THIS JOB?

RELIEF! Thank Christ! There's somebody else in the world who thinks you should be able to make a decent living selling funny words on paper.

WHAT IF YOU'RE WRONG? Then you'll have people to talk to in the soup line. In the meantime, they'll pay you.

That sounds good, but **DO YOU THINK I'M QUALIFIED?**

Probably. You've been writing humor for twenty years. Not everybody gets pieces into *The New Yorker* and on SNL.

For God's sake don't tell Knock Knock that. Maybe they'll be impressed. Some of those pieces were graphic, too—remember that Periodic Table? Or the parody of *The Wall Street Journal*?

I'm not a designer, though. For example, I don't think these typefaces are quite right. The grid's not the same. And this isn't really a decision tree, it's just a conversation.

OH, THOSE PEOPLE ARE ALL **KNUCKLEHEADS.**

It would be nice to learn design from people who really know their stuff.

Well, maybe you should've actually bought the Tufte rather than just browsing it at Hennessy & Ingalls…Even if Knock Knock never calls you, they'll appreciate the effort.

OR: THEY'LL THINK I'M A TOTAL FREAK.

Better they should find out now, no?

That's the spirit. You even own some Knock Knock products, don't you?

Yeah, their takeout menu holder. And my wife Kate buys their post-its.

THAT'S A REASON RIGHT THERE: if they had you in for an interview, you could probably swipe a couple of things for Kate. Security is probably quite lax.

Point taken, but what could be better than working from home, writing novels? I set my own schedule, I'm my own boss—

I hate to break it to you, but **YOUR BOSS IS AN A-HOLE.**

Watch your mouth! This is a family cover letter.

Don't evade. You work constantly. Maybe if you work in an office again you'll, I dunno, **GET A LIFE?**

Yeah but here, I don't even have to take a shower.

That's a good thing? Look, it wouldn't harm you to get out of the house. You're so bored you're **EATING TEASPOONS OF RAW HORSERADISH.**

You've been spying on me again!

The screams give you away.

OH YES, ALL MY DECISIONS ARE THIS TORTURED. WHY DO YOU ASK?

But…what about the cats?

Excuse me, but I did I just hear you say, **"WHAT ABOUT THE CATS?"** Screw them! What have those little vandals ever done for you? Circle you begging for food, then puke all over everything? They're precisely the reason you should interview for this Editor job. If you think you're getting your security deposit back, you're deluded.

Money's OK. My Harry Potter parodies—

Look, you like their stuff, their office is in Venice, and they're looking for an editor…Imagine working on a decent computer. Your Mac puts the "crep" in "decrepit." You're applying for this job. It's basically what you do anyway.

You guess? Last Fall—while you were revising a novel, running a group blog, and supervising a redesign of your old college humor magazine—you wrote a parody of Dickens, made it look like the 1843 edition of *A Christmas Carol*, and sent it to all your friends. Juggling multiple projects, working with a staff, supervising all phases of production… This is what you do all day, every day.

I guess. I'm the world's worst job-hunter.

That Jen person did seem nice from what I read on the internet, and **"HOW TO FIND TRUE LOVE" IS MAGNIFICENT.**

You can bike to Jody Maroni's after and drown your sorrows in sausage. At the very least, you'll know a few more interesting people.

Fine! I'll send a **RESUMÉ.**

And a Periodic Table.

I said I would do it, all right?

No need to get tense, just trying to help…Now, was that so difficult?

ARE YOU KIDDING?

michaelagerber@gmail.com
(310) 458-0454

3

TABLE OF CONTENTS

"You're trending—what the hell have you been up to?"

DEPARTMENTS
Frontispiece: "Mondrian's Map of Colorado" **by Ron Hauge**... 1
Publisher's Letter **by Michael Gerber** 2
Modern Mythology #3: "Lotta and the Swan" **by Jim Siergey** 8
Spotlight: Criminal Mischief **by Nick Downes**........ 10
"A Day In the Life of a Surrealist" **by Ron Barrett**........ 76

GALLIMAUFRY
Django Gold, Chris Galletta, Jeff Kulik, John McNamee, Oscar Rhea, Ryan Standfest, Maryann Corbett, Ali Solomon, Clarke Jaxton Motorbike, Anthony Scibelli, Sarah Totton, Eva Meckna, Luis Leal Miranda, Jon Savitt, Jonathan Zeller, E.R. Flynn, Hilary Allison, Stan Mack, Steve Jones, Matt Dooman, Michael Pershan, Rose Boyle.

SHORT STUFF
Y2K **by K.A. Polzin**........ 21
The Shitth Stage of Grief **by Neil Mitchell** 22
A Press Conference About This Morning Where I Was Going to Get So Much Done **by Daniel Lavery** 24
Please Remember to RSVP! **by Charlie Hankin**........ 26
Endangered Beetle **by Simon Rich**........ 28

FEATURES
The Tabby **by Drew Dernavich**........ 31
The Lost Mall of Atlanta **by Brian McConnachie** 32
Three Cartoons **by M.K. Brown** 35

The AMERICAN BYSTANDER
Founded 1981 by Brian McConnachie
#21 • Vol. 6, No. 1 • November 2021

EDITOR & PUBLISHER Michael Gerber
HEAD WRITER Brian McConnachie
SENIOR EDITOR Alan Goldberg
ORACLE Steve Young
STAFF LIAR P.S. Mueller
INTREPID TRAVELER Mike Reiss
EAGLE EYES Patrick L. Kennedy
TWOFIFTYONE.NET Chase/Doyle/Nink
AGENTS OF THE 2ND BYSTANDER INT'L
Eve Alintuck, Melissa Balmain, Ron Barrett, Roz Chast, Rick Geary, Sam Gross
MANAGING EDITOR EMERITA Jennifer Finney Boylan
CONSIGLIERA Kate Powers
COVER BY Blitt

ISSUE CONTRIBUTORS
Hilary Allison, Ian Baker, Mat Barton, Lou Beach, R.O. Blechman, Barry Blitt, George Booth, Rose Boyle, M.K. Brown, Eddie Campbell, T.Q. Chen, Tom Chitty, Adam Cooper, Maryann Corbett, Drew Dernavich, Matt Dooman, Nick Downes, Bob Eckstein, Emily Flake, Shary Flenniken, E.R. Flynn, Chris Galletta, Lucas Gardner, Django Gold, Charlie Hankin, Lance Hansen, Todd Hanson, Ron Hauge, Brandon Hicks, Steve Jones, Ben Kawaller, Jeff Kulik, Daniel Lavery, Stan Mack, Ross MacDonald, John McNamee, Merrill Markoe, Eva Meckna, Neil Mitchell, Luis Miranda, Clarke Jaxton Motorbike, Oliver Ottitsch, Michael Pershan, K.A. Polzin, Oscar Rhee, Simon Rich, Jon Savitt, Anthony Scibelli, Jim Siergey, Ali Solomon, Rick Sparks, Nick Spooner, Ryan Standfest, Sarah Totton, Dalton Vaughn, D. Watson, & Jonathan Zeller.

Lanky Bareikis, Jon Schwarz, Alleen Schultz, Gray & Bernstein, Lopez, Ivanhoe & Gumenick, Greg & Trish, Kelsey Hoke.
NAMEPLATES BY Mark Simonson
ISSUE CREATED BY Michael Gerber

Vol. 6, No. 1. ©2021 Good Cheer LLC, all rights reserved. Produced in weirdly damp Santa Monica, California, USA.

He was a Jewish kid from Brooklyn on his way to becoming the NFL's first great quarterback.

His father was the mobbed-up killer of his own brother-in-law, a murder that made headlines in New York City for years.

Sid Luckman would end up in the Pro Football Hall of Fame while his father became a secret he kept forever, even from his own children. **Until now.**

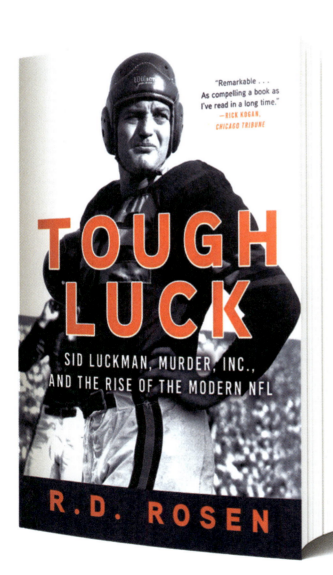

TOUGH LUCK
SID LUCKMAN, MURDER, INC., AND THE RISE OF THE MODERN NFL
by R.D. ROSEN

"... a great and beautifully written untold story." —GAY TALESE

"A magnificent book."
—MARV LEVY, PRO FOOTBALL HALL OF FAME COACH

"Remarkable. . . . As compelling a book as I've read in a long time." —RICK KOGAN, *CHICAGO TRIBUNE* AND WGN RADIO

"With great research and storytelling, Rosen brings to life Depression-era New York and WWII-era Chicago in **a wonderful family saga that will captivate history and sports fan alike.**"
—PUBLISHERS WEEKLY

AVAILABLE AT ALL BOOKSELLERS

Meanwhile…in Feudal Japan **by Oliver Ottitsch** 36
All Clear **by Todd Hanson** 37
A Brief History of the Hat-Bot **by Tom Chitty** 41
What I Had Done for Love **by Ben Kawaller** 42
Amagola **by Lou Beach** 46
"Your Aunt Kate" **by Eddie Campbell** 48
Heavenly Passages **by R.O. Blechman** 53
Three Cartoons **by Rich Sparks** 55
Never Good Enough **by Shary Flenniken** 56
Saturdays **by Alan Goldberg** 58
Three Cartoons **by Nick Spooner** 60
The Yoga of Group Dog-Walking **by Merrill Markoe** 61
HUGE FAN! **by D. Watson** 62
Anxiety! **by Dalton Vaughn** 63
The Gnome **by Brandon Hicks** 65

OUR BACK PAGES

Notes From a Small Planet **by Rick Geary** 69
What Am I Doing Here? **by Mike Reiss** 71
Daybreak and a Candle-End **by Ron Barrett** 73
Roz's Marvelous Collages **by Roz Chast** 74
P.S. Mueller Thinks Like This **by P.S. Mueller** 75

CARTOONS & ILLUSTRATIONS BY

Ian Baker, Barry Blitt, George Booth, Sam Gross, Nick Downes, John McNamee, Ali Solomon, Hilary Allison, Steve Jones, Emily Flake, Dalton Vaughn, Charlie Hankin, Lance Hansen, Ross MacDonald, Bob Eckstein, K.A. Polzin, Lars Kenseth, T.Q. Chen, Cooper & Barton, Tom Chitty, Lou Beach, Kate Carew, Rick Geary.

Sam's Spot

"What happened?"

COVER

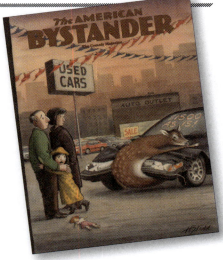

HARRY BLISS provides the perfect introduction to this slightly bigger issue—what you might call a Holiday "bumper crop." Harry's our first two-time cover artist, a very happy thing indeed. Deep thanks to him, and don't worry little girl—it's just a *cartoon* deer.

ACKNOWLEDGMENTS

All material is ©2021 its creators, all rights reserved. Please do not reproduce or distribute any of it without written consent of the creators and *The American Bystander*. The following material has previously appeared, and is reprinted here with permission of the author(s): "Never Good Enough" originally appeared in *The Dreadfuls Special* published by Rotland Press, available from rotlandpress.com.

THE AMERICAN BYSTANDER, Vol. 6, No. 1, (978-0-578-33188-1). Publishes ~4x/year. ©2021 by Good Cheer LLC. No part of this magazine can be reproduced, in whole or in part, by any means, without the written permission of the Publisher. For this and other queries, email Publisher@americanbystander.org, or write: Michael Gerber, Publisher, *The American Bystander*, 1122 Sixth St., #403, Santa Monica, CA 90403. Single copies can be purchased at www.americanbystander.org/store. **Subscribe at www.patreon.com/bystander.** Other info—probably more than anyone could possibly require—can be found on our website, www.americanbystander.org. Thankee for reading.

Lotta and the Swan

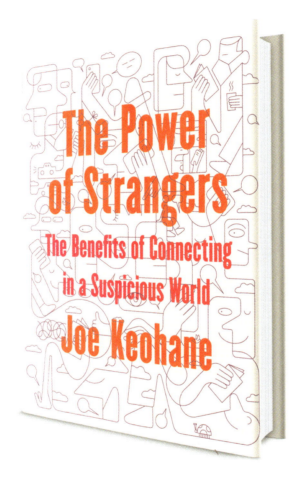

SIX OF THE BEST
BY NICK DOWNES
CRIMINAL MISCHIEF
The lighter side of the larcenous life

"You never get used to this sort of mayhem."

"Look, honey—clowns!"

"These days, Harry and I are just living from forged check to forged check."

"You can turn off the Magic Fingers."

"He's an obvious flight risk, your honor."

NICK DOWNES *lays low in Brooklyn, NY.*

STAFF
Gallimaufry

FILM CRITICS REVIEW MY LOVEMAKING ABILITIES.

"Exhilarating! Django delivers a forceful, energetic performance that starts out strong and doesn't let up until an explosive climax. A must-experience!"
—Lisa Kennedy, *The Denver Post*

"Remarkable! Serves up a nonstop barrage of pulse-pounding action that had me on the edge of my seat for the entire 90 minutes!"
—Dana Stevens, *Slate*

"Tremendous! Gold is masterful at what he does and once again left this critic out of breath and eager to go again. This is one thrill ride that the whole family will enjoy!"
—Richard Brody, *The New Yorker*

"How dare you! How dare you attempt to degrade this, transform a moment of intimacy into some salacious broadsheet blurb, shamble into my heart for more of these cheap, winking entendres. You people sicken me. My review is this: When I was on my back, with my blouse open and his hot cock curling up inside me, we were in union. Two bodies, one breath, the world far away. There, then, I felt safe. Safe! Do you know what that's like? *Could* you?"
—Janet Maslin, *The New York Times*

"Incredible! Easily the most fun I had in a movie theater this year!"
—Richard Roeper, *Chicago Sun-Times*

—*Django Gold*

SOME FESTIVE SEASONAL CANDLES.

Leafy Miasma
Enforced Apple Picking
Plunging Your Face into Tim Burton's Hair
Black Tea with Cloves Poured Hot by Your Aunt Who Stormed the Capitol
Cinnamon Apocalypse
Smoldering "Live Laugh Love" Sign
The Inside of Michael Myers's Mask
Overheated Facebook Server
Whiskey, Oak and Testosterone Supplements
Pumpkin Cinnamon Chai Blah Blah Bullshit Bullshit

—*Chris Galletta*

THE CAST OF *YANKEE DOODLE DANDY*—WHERE ARE THEY NOW?

The inimitable James Cagney—dead
The lovely Joan Leslie—dead
The powerful Walter Huston—dead
The criminally underrated Richard Whorf—dead
The always charming Irene Manning—dead
The instantly recognizable George Tobias—dead
The adorable child star Douglas Croft—dead since 1963
The effervescent Rosemary DeCamp—dead

—*Jeff Kulik*

SANDWICHED IN TIME.

Me = starving, about to eat a sandwich
Future Me = stepping through a glowing rift in space and time
Me: Hey, you look familiar.
Future Me: I'm you from the future and there's no time to explain! Don't eat that sandwich!
Me: Why?
Future Me: There's no time to explain! If you eat that sandwich terrible things will happen!
Me: What terrible things?
Future Me: What part of "there's no time to explain" don't you understand?
Me: Wait a minute: if you know that terrible things will happen then you must have eaten this sandwich,

"Early trials show our invisibility serum to be over 95% effective."

THE AMERICAN MATCHBOOK COMPANY

by Ryan Standfest

and you turned out fine.
Future Me: Fine? Do I look fine to you? I'm begging you: if you care at all about your future well-being, you will give me that sandwich immediately!
Me: What are you going to do with it?
Future Me: I'm going to banish it into the future, where it will become nothing but harmless ham and cheese once again.
Me = reluctantly giving Future Me the sandwich
Future Me: You've made the right choice. Farewell!
Future Me = disappearing back through the glowing rift
Me: That was strange…I'm starving…I wish I had a sandwich…
Me = looking at the glowing rift, shrugging, stepping through.
Past Me = starving, about to eat a sandwich
Past Me: Hey, you look familiar.
Me: I'm you from the future and there's no time to explain! Don't eat that sandwich!

—*Oscar Rhea*

ELEGY FOR THE MURDER MYSTERY'S SECOND VICTIM.

Where have we seen you before?
Was it some other Britbox concoction
splattering gore on our brains,
streaming last year, or last week?
Always the bald one, the fat one,
the weak-in-the-chin, or the frumpy,
bosomy-giggly-and-vain, or
spectacled-mousy-and-meek,

off you go, drunkenly bumbling
into the dark, while a chorus
   cues us that murder impends
(Verdi or Mozart or Bach).
And there are the leather-gloved hands
that will lunge from a lurk in the bushes,
   striking before you can gasp.
   Or maybe they're picking the lock

into your entryway, waiting, with crowbars or knives or syringes.
   Whomp. And the music goes manic.
   A shot of your agonized mug
ends it: your role in the drama,
your bit in the red-herring subplot,
   thread that we'll lose by the end,
   dumped in the tangle. We shrug,

but maybe we shiver a little—a judder,
a jar to the psyche—
   seeing you've slid out of mind, after
   the credit list rolls.
You will rise up to new death!
in new series and seasons and stories.
   We will stay dead. We'll be stuck
   with our frumpy, forgettable souls.

—*Maryann Corbett*

I THINK MY GIRLFRIEND IS ABOUT TO BREAK UP WITH ME.

When we watch a movie, instead of cuddling with me, she cuddles with a big Ed Hardy t-shirt she stuffed with leaves.

Whenever we make out, she says it'd be cool if we didn't use our hands or mouths or skin. We just sit next to each other sort of wiggling.

I asked her over the phone if she wanted to go roller skating. She was like, "Of course." But then she hung up. Later I saw pictures on social media of her roller skating alone.

On my birthday, she gave me a bicycle, which was nice. Except she kept referring to it as a "one person" bicycle.

She has started introducing me to her friends as one of her mom's coworkers.

At the carnival we got stuck at the top of the Ferris wheel. I thought it was romantic, but as soon as the ride stopped, she started constructing a hang glider out of her jacket. The messed-up thing is it worked. She coasted down to the ground and I didn't see her again until later. When I found her, she was eating two caramel apples and didn't offer me a bite of either.

When I asked her if she wanted to go to couple's therapy, she seemed to grow pensive before telling me that while she and the Ed Hardy t-shirt had ups and downs, she was confident they could work it out on their own.

—*Clarke Jaxton Motorbike*

THE TRUTH IS OUT THERE.

I knew my boss wouldn't believe me if I said I was late for work because I was abducted by aliens, because what are the odds of that happening twice in one week?

—*Anthony Scibelli*

SLOGANS FOR DUCK MILK.

Duck milk: Because she's worth it.
Duck milk: The only milk you need.
Duck milk: A party in your cereal. A revolution in your mouth.
Duck milk: For strong bones and beaks. Got duck?
Everybody loves duck milk. Is this amazing or is this amazing?
Every day they're out there making duck milk! Woo-oo!
Venice. Zurich. Paris. Duck milk.
Got a match? Game, set, duck milk.
Duck milk: The other white milk.

—*Sarah Totton*

THE A.K.C. RECOGNIZES SEVEN NEW BREEDS.

The Bowlegged Squatter
The Greater Canadian Bakun Trawler
The Toy Würstchenhund
The Perrier Terrier
The Allegheny Strutter
The Giant Albanian Molardog
The Coarsemouthed Boozhound

—*Eva Meckna*

I'M GOING TO BUILD A TIME MACHINE.

I'm going to build a time machine to go back in time and slap the guy who, many years ago, came out of a time machine and slapped me.

—*Luis Leal Miranda*

REJECTED HGTV SHOWS.

Yep, That's a House!
Open Concept, Open Marriage
Frankie Muniz Used to Live Here
The Price Is Low Because Someone Was Murdered

—*Jon Savitt*

A BIG QUESTION.

When I was six and we were on our way to temple, I asked Dad if God was real. He said: "I don't know." He didn't know! That really impacted me. A few years later, I met a guy who did know that God was real, and I joined his cult.

—*Jonathan Zeller*

A Fetish For Finance
by E.R. Flynn

BILBO BAGGINS SAYS GOODBYE TO THE DWARVES, AS HE HEADS BACK TO THE SHIRE.

Bilbo: I will miss you all. What a wonderful adventure this was. So long, Dori. Ori. Nori....'Big Guy.' Oin. Gloin.
"Excuse me. What was that?"
Bilbo: Just saying goodbye.
"You don't know my name, do you?"
Bilbo: What? Of course, I know your name. I know all the dwarves' names. Don't be ridiculous.
"What is it then?"
Bilbo: Hmm. What was that?
"I can't believe you don't know my name after this whole adventure. I rode with you on the back of a giant eagle."
Bilbo: I remember it well.
"Saved you from a Goblin."
Bilbo: For which I'm eternally grateful.
"Helped you kill a giant spider."
Bilbo: Of course you did. We fought the giant spider together, you and I.
"I was bluffing. [points] He's the one that killed the spider with you."
Bilbo: ...
"You have no idea who any of us are."
(A pause.)
(Bilbo slips on the Ring and disappears.)
(Sound of footsteps speeding away.)
—Anthony Scibelli

"REMOTE MAN," THE NEW SUPERHERO WHO HELPS KIDS WITH THE HARD LEVELS.

INT. CHILD'S BEDROOM — DAY
Sam: Aw man, what the heck. I can't beat this level!
A crash is heard. SAM turns around to see that his bedroom wall has been reduced to rubble. REMOTE MAN is standing in the wreckage, hands on hips.
Remote Man: Did someone say, "Aw man, what the heck. I cannot beat this level?"
SAM cheers.
REMOTE MAN sits down and silently plays through the entirety of Metroid Prime. The room around

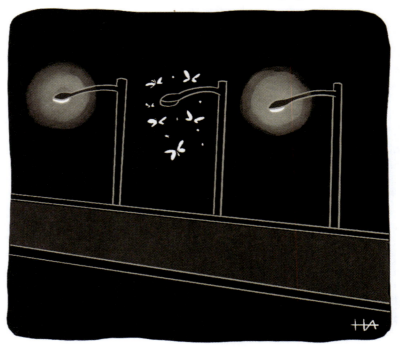

GOTH MOTHS

THE LIFE OF HE.

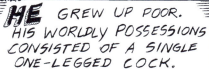

HE GREW UP POOR. HIS WORLDLY POSSESSIONS CONSISTED OF A SINGLE ONE-LEGGED COCK.

AS A BOY HE COULD OUTRUN THEM ALL — AS LONG AS HE CLAIMED TO BE HARD OF HEARING.

HE GREW VERY TALL. AND AS WITH ALL TALL KIDS HE LOVED TO HIDE BEHIND SMALL OBJECTS AND JUMP OUT AT THEM.

WHEN HE WAS GROWN, HE BUILT A SQUARE HOME WITH TWENTY CORNERS. HE BUILT A FENCE TO CONTAIN THE BIRDS AND DUG A LAKE TO HOLD THE MOON.

THEY ATTACKED THE NEXT MORNING. HE DISLOCATED HIS BACK WHEN HE TRIED TO TIP A TRENCH OVER ON THEM...

AFTER THE SLAUGHTER THE DEAD GOT UP, BRUSHED THEMSELVES OFF, AND WENT HOME.

HE CONSULTED A MADMAN FOR TREATMENT.

THE MADMAN TOLD HIM TO GET INTO BED AND STAY THERE — UNTIL THE TREES TURN TO IRON.

AND NOW HE DRINKS — A LITTLE — AND WORRIES ABOUT GETTING BALD...

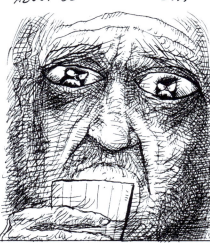

©stan mack

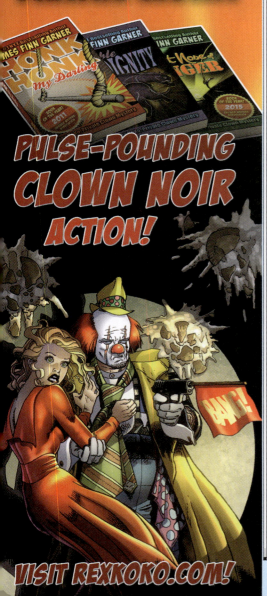

"YA CAN'T PUT A PRICE ON MONEY."

The sawdust-n-tinsel ghetto of Top Town ain't a Sunday School show, pally. Danger hangs in the air like the smell of popcorn, whiskey and fear. When the heat comes down on this mob of circus has-beens, there's only one joey you can trust:

REX KOKO
PRIVATE CLOWN

PULSE-POUNDING CLOWN NOIR ACTION!

VISIT REXKOKO.COM!

"Do you think we've lost the ability to enjoy the finer things in life?"

them continues to crumble, as the wall REMOTE MAN destroyed was load-bearing.
Sam: Wow, Remote Man, you're great!
Remote Man: Ha, ha!
REMOTE MAN exits through the destroyed wall and jogs across the street, causing a five-car pile-up.
FIN

—*Matt Dooman*

ABOUT THE MURDERER.

Michael Pershan is a teacher, writer and murderer. His debut murder, of former best friend and personal trainer Danny, was named Best New Murder by the New York Police Department. His current murder is the first in a planned trilogy. There were also prequels, you'll never find the bodies. He lives with his family and children in New York City.

—*Michael Pershan*

THINGS MY DAD SAID TO ME AFTER I LOST THE BIG GAME THAT I'LL NEVER FORGET.

1. "Nice win, kid." (Resumes work call.)
2. Listen, you just gotta march onto that court, pick the biggest kid and tell him you're going to beat his ass. And then ya do it. On the court or on the blacktop. Any which way. And if you can't do it? Well, then I suggest you apologize. For lying.
3. You see those vertical lines on the side of the mountain? Those are blast holes from the charges they used to clear the way for this road. Real dynamite. Like in the cartoons.
4. I oughta have you talk to my Uncle Zoom. He was a natural. And boy could he dance…Man did the worm so dirty, it got clean.
5. Boy, what I wouldn't give to see the outtakes from that *Survivor* show.
6. Welp, winning isn't everything. Krispy Kreme, on the other hand…What's say we get a Krispy Kreme?
7. That Dale's a real champion. What's his Dad-situation? I bet he already has one, right?
8. Your sister was in a skiing accident.

—*Rose Boyle*

WARNING! WARNING! WARNING! Much of this material first appeared on twofiftyone.net, *Bystander*'s website for short stuff. It's edited by Adam Chase, Ben Doyle and Jonah Nink, and is POWERFULLY ADDICTIVE.

"Sippy tries to warn them all—he knows the bags are trouble!

But underwater, as a straw, his voice is just a bubble."

"An instant classic."
—STEVE BRODNER

"A powerful lesson wrapped in endless charm...beautifully conceived, written and illustrated."
—RON HAUGE

"The Last Straw is a lovely book—a sweet eco-tale rendered in obsessive, passionate detail."
—BARRY BLITT

• • • • • •

Artist **ZOE MATTHIESSEN** takes on the plastic problem in her debut children's book **THE LAST STRAW**

• • • • • •

www.SippyTheLastStraw.com
www.NorthAtlanticBooks.com

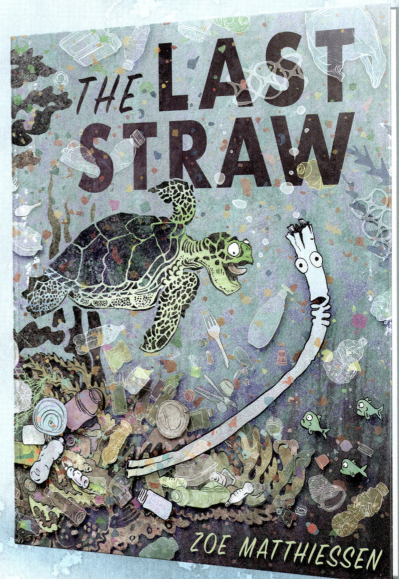

WHERE WERE YOU IN '92?

USED

SLOUCHERS

A NOVEL BY E.L. LESSERT

BASED ON THE SCREENPLAY BY MAC MCHENRY

Out Now

BY MIKE SACKS

NOSTALGIA
BY K.A. POLZIN
Y2K
An episode from American History

IT WAS 1999. ALL THAT YEAR, TENSION HAD BEEN BUILDING. NEWS REPORTS CLAIMED THAT, DUE TO A PROGRAMMING GLITCH, ON NEW YEAR'S EVE, COMPUTERS WORLDWIDE COULD MALFUNCTION, CAUSING GLOBAL CHAOS: AIRPLANES WOULD FALL FROM THE SKY; NUCLEAR MISSILES WOULD LAUNCH THEMSELVES; GEOCITIES WOULD BE INACCESSIBLE.

THE SCARIEST PART: NO ONE COULD PREDICT THE EXTENT OF THE CHAOS. WE ONLY KNEW THAT IF COMPUTERS FAILED TO NAVIGATE THE CHANGE FROM 1999 TO 2000, ALL COULD BE LOST. THAT YEAR, BUNKER CONSTRUCTION SKYROCKETED. FRIGHTENED CITIZENS STOCKPILED FOOD, SUPPLIES, AND AS ALWAYS, GUNS. FEAR WAS IN THE AIR.

MEANWHILE, BUSINESSES WORLDWIDE HAD BEEN WORKING TO SECURE THEIR COMPUTER SYSTEMS, AN UNSEXY STORY THAT FAILED TO GRAB THE HEADLINES. SO WHEN THE CRITICAL MOMENT ARRIVED, THERE WAS MINIMAL TO NO CHAOS. A VIDEO STORE CUSTOMER WAS BILLED FOR 100 YEARS OF LATE FEES (BUT SURVIVED). SOME CASH REGISTER RECEIPTS IN GREECE HAD A DATE OF "1900," POTENTIALLY AFFECTING ALIBIS.

THE ONLY DEATHS WERE OF PEOPLE WHO WERE GOING TO DIE ANYWAY (R.I.P.). TODAY, Y2K IS LARGELY REMEMBERED AS AN OVER-REACTION, A FALSE ALARM, RATHER THAN AS THE I.T. SUCCESS STORY IT REALLY WAS. "BETTER TO BE AN ANONYMOUS SUCCESS THAN A PUBLIC FAILURE," SOMEONE SAID.

K.A. POLZIN
(Instagram: @k.a.polzin) is a writer & cartoonist. He amassed his vast wealth as a kindergarten teacher. People just assume he knows karate.

"SITTING SHIVA"
BY NEIL MITCHELL
THE SHITTH STAGE OF GRIEF
Sasipgujae *and* karoshi *in the realm of the Superior Being*

My wife Leah passed away recently. Despite five years of a breast cancer diagnosis, I found myself unprepared. My sorrow is constant, in ways unexpected and profound. Our goal was always survival, so her death felt sudden, unforeseen.

Leah and I did, however, have many discussions about how I should leave my unfulfilling job after her passing. She wanted for me what I want for myself: to explore my creativity and an artistic vocation, escaping the pursuit of corporate profits benefitting an employer and its clients neither of which I care about.

My happiness was important to her, but today I returned to my office, grief-stricken and defeated. Back in Manhattan in a 20th floor office, each moment ushers in a new phase—re-connection, betrayal, normalcy.

It is now 1:45pm. My grief deepens, and impairs my commitment to effective media consulting. The Buddhists have the tradition of *sasipgujae* that commemorates the 49th day after death as the end of the mourning period. I, having returned to my life as a soulless New York City office drone, inaugurate my own tradition: taking a shit in our floor's shared office bathroom.

Enthroned, pants at knees, I am inspired by two complementary Japanese traditions: death haiku and bowel movement poetry.

"Meeting Respite"
(Setsuko Otani, 1952)
Cold stall, cavernous
Seat uncomfortably moist
My superior's

The inter-office bathroom, a temple of shame and overshared vulnerability, is for those shallow in pride; only the bold dare enter the glistening enamelled sanctum where your CEO could unexpectedly drop in just to brush his teeth.

Heavy with symbolism and Shake Shack, the body warms the seat. The posterior dries unforeseen and unidentifiable wetness. This ritual serves to replace pain as the unwelcomed element the body must now absorb.

Leaning forward, the bereaved places his head in his hands. This act of prayer triggers the automated flush mechanism. This will be the first of four automated flushes that mirror the rote repetition inherent in *karoshi*, Japanese for "death by overwork."

Having wiped, my slate is clean. I pause in a meditative state that will, in coming days, evolve to the advanced pose of "toilet naps." In this twilight condition, the "living" must reacquaint themselves with this seat that has hosted sleep, tears and mournful whispers of "What the fuck am I doing with my life?"

My life's purpose may indeed be to figure just what the fuck it is I really am doing with my life. Leah certainly couldn't explain it at a party. Perhaps it is our shared inability to understand how talent, intelligence and white privilege could be so perfectly squandered that will forever bind Leah and me together.

I zip up. The scent of death hangs in the air. Leftover droplets of urine dribble upon the thigh, summoning the remembrance of laundry, a ritual unlikely to occur. The toll of the fourth flush signifies that the wetly Raptured feces will now commune with others who have left the body. And also rats.

The clang of the unlocked stall betokens I am free. Somewhat. My thoughts drift to what would be a good time for a coffee break. Perhaps 3:00 or 3:15? I consider the stamina of both body and soul.

As is customary, a Superior Being enters. He is the new VP of Gaming. He is followed by a stranger from the adjacent office, that company that seems like a front for oil crimes and has a logo resembling a Golan-Globus hieroglyph on a 1986 VHS box (see the sacred death art of the *Texas Chainsaw Massacre 2* packaging for reference). My bereavement leave prevented our meeting, so the new VP (we now have 20) and I exchange mortification, our ceremonial greeting hygienically inconvenienced. Handshake forsaken, the VP and I express only words. Words that ease my self-disappointment and somewhere must be amusing to Leah in their unintentional humor. The depth of meaning in my sentiments, simultaneously shared by the Gaming VP, are manifold: "I'm sorry we had to meet under these circumstances."

NEIL MITCHELL (@NRMdom) *is a writer and filmmaker based in Staten Island, where Midwestern transplants are called "nice" but are misunderstood.*

ACCOUNTABILITY

BY DANIEL LAVERY

A PRESS CONFERENCE ABOUT WHAT HAPPENED THIS MORNING WHERE I WAS GOING TO GET SO MUCH DONE

Good morning. Thank you all for coming on such short notice. Let's g— you're right, of course. My mistake. I do apologize.
[Pause for question, inaudible.]
Yes, that is exactly the kind of thing that we've been talking about. Yes. Mm-hmm.
[Pause for question, inaudible.]
Yes, I do agree it's representative of the larger problem. Good afternoon. It's afternoon now. Slip of the tongue, won't happen again.
[Pause for question, inaudible.]
Yes, this morning got away from us. That's why we called this presser today, in the interest of full transparency and for the purpose of ensuring this sort of thing doesn't happen again tomorrow, or whenever the next chunk of time is expected to arrive.
[Pause for question, inaudible.]
I don't know. That seems like a question for shipping or receivables. I don't know the answer to that. What I can tell you is this: We started the day with the best of intentions and with a realistic plan for success. We were here, we were prepared, we absolutely showed up to win.
[Pause for question, inaudible.]
I'd like to clarify that we did wake up on time, for whatever it's worth. Not that we're making excuses. There are no excuses for what happened out there this morning. But we did actually wake up on time, right when the alarm went off, and we didn't go back to sleep or anything.
[Pause for question, inaudible.]
The plan was to start at 9:00.
[Pause for question, inaudible.]
Like I said, the plan was to start at 9:00. I can't speak to all the whys or wherefores of that. What I can tell you—what I've already told you, but which I'm happy to repeat again because, like I said, we're interested in complete transparency—is that somewhere in between "waking up on time," "not going back to sleep," and "getting started at 9:00," something else happened.
[Pause for question, inaudible.]
[*Shortly*] I don't know. I must have blacked out.
[Pause for question, inaudible.]
Yes, I'm sorry. That was rude. My apologies. I don't mean to take this out on you. In bed, obviously, and it's possible that after turning off the alarm, the phone continued to be looked at, continued to be on, and there was scrolling. Likely there was scrolling, yes. I can tell you I was out of bed at 10:10, although I don't think that move was permanent. I think I got up and out of bed a few times before I got all the way out of bed, like, for the day, if that's what you mean. The first cup of tea was definitely underway before 10.
[Pause for question, inaudible.]
How many?
[Pause for question, inaudible.]
You'd have to ask someone else on the team that question.
[Pause for question, inaudible.]
You mean tea and coffee both, inclusive? We keep different records for tea and coffee. You'd have to ask the coffee guy about that. I know I had one cup of tea for sure. But I usually reuse that cup for future cups of tea, so I couldn't tell you offhand how many times it got reused that morning.
[Pause for question, inaudible.]
Yes, this morning got away from us. We weren't out of bed at 9:00. If I were to guess—I don't like to guess, I'd rather wait until more of the numbers came in, but if we're just talking about a back-of-the-envelope sketch, I'd say that when we

DANIEL LAVERY *wrote the books* Something That May Shock and Discredit You, The Merry Spinster, *and* Texts From Jane Eyre, *cofounded* The Toast *and runs* The Chatner *weekly newsletter.*

realized it was 9:00 all of a sudden, even though we'd woken up on time at 8:15 and hadn't done anything since 8:15, so how can you suddenly tell me it's 45 minutes later when nothing has happened? If you wake up at 8:15 and then nothing happens and suddenly it's 9:12, what are you supposed to do with that? How are you supposed to develop any sort of meaningful relationship between time and effect, between external and internal signifiers of timeliness—seasonableness—between will and action, between the body and the world the body moves through? You tell me. You tell me that, okay. You go tell those kids in the locker room who just put everything out on the line that actually no time has passed at all, because sometimes you don't do anything and time passes, and sometimes you do as much as you can and time doesn't pass, and you go explain that to them.

[Pause for question, inaudible.]

I would have marked the period between 8:15 and 9:12 as waking up slowly, which is a value of mine, and so anything that occurred during that period would have been filed under just generally waking up. The process of waking up. Which takes time, you can't just—you can't just flip a switch. And then you're trying to get your arms wrapped around the day, you're trying to get a hold of something real, but the morning is just featureless, like a big wet rock face and you're climbing barefoot. My best guess is that when we realized 9:00 had already come and gone that the best thing to do, the safest thing to do, in the interest of safety, was to hang tight in the same place and wait for the next round number to come around before trying to start anything new.

[Pause for question, inaudible.]

You ever try to start something new at 17 minutes after the hour, son? You ever seen what that does to the human body? If you'd seen that, you wouldn't be asking me that question. I've seen it.

[Pause for question, inaudible.]

I think I already conceded that point.

[Pause for question, inaudible.]

Listen, the morning is gone and it's not coming back. There might have been a window of opportunity shortly before 10, but that was when we learned there was a delivery coming at 11—that was supposed to arrive at 11—I don't know, we still haven't heard, I think they don't have my new number yet so actually I should probably go see if I can log into the client portal and try to update it, as long as there's no two-step verification—obviously there was no chance of starting something new at 10 with that going on, so—The morning is gone. Okay? And I'm as sorry about that as anyone, but it's just gone. But this afternoon's not going to get away from us.

[Pause for question, inaudible.]

Well, we've got a plan.

[Pause for question, inaudible.]

Hey, hey. Hey! Settle down. Settle down, all right, one at a time—If you would just let us explain the plan, we could execute the plan—

[Pause for question, inaudible.]

It's after what?

[Pause for question, inaudible.]

Well, shit. I don't know. Seems like the safest thing to do now is just wait until evening when we can reset the clock, try getting something done then.

[Pause for question, inaudible.]

I don't know, five? Evening starts at five? That seems fair. Morning is morning, mid-morning is 9 to 10:50, late morning is a little hard to pin down, noon isn't anything, doesn't count, can't be lunch because morning didn't start until 9 but it's when everyone else is doing lunch so it's ghost lunch, then sometimes things can happen at 1, but then 2-3:30 is lunch on account of missing lunch earlier, which means 4 is too heavy, and then 5 is evening, I think. Yeah, five's evening, seven's supper, nine is for remembering things from 2, and then ten is night.

[Pause for question, inaudible.]

Wait until five, I guess. What takes two hours to do?

[Pause for question, inaudible.]

You're putting me on. Seriously? We just sat down five minutes ago.

[Pause for question, inaudible.]

No kidding? Okay, five more minutes of questions, then, that should eat up about two hours and then we can try kicking off the morning again at 5 p.m. sharp. Someone set an alarm so I don't forget, hands up where I can see 'em—yeah, blue shirt, third row, what's your question?

A MALIGN FÊTE
BY CHARLIE HANKIN
Please remember to RSVP!

A tip: launch iPhone's "Roentgen Monitor" before approaching 833 N. Elm.

This is just a gentle reminder, if you haven't already, to RSVP for Ashley's and my thing!! We just need an exact head count so we can shop accordingly. And great news—Ashley is making her world-famous Pecan Dindles!

Please see the attached map for location information. For those of you who haven't been to our place (welcome!), we are a bit tucked away. Here at 833 1/2 N. Elm, we are rather hidden behind 833 N. Elm. Do not go to 833 N. Elm. 833 N. Elm—red brick, octagonal, surrounded by dead birds—belongs to our landlord, Dr. Ledarius, and is a trap. We love Dr. Ledarius, and he has worked very hard on the "irreversibility field" surrounding 833 N. Elm, so we do not want to annoy him by touching it!! Also we will be unable to retrieve you from 833 N. Elm.

By the way, this soiree will be strictly BYOB. We have some stuff here (wine, beer, a small but TASTY selection of spirits Ashley brought back from Cannes) but we will not be sharing :(

Let us know in advance if you have any pet allergies. We have two tiny but affectionate Italian greyhounds, and a third affectionate Italian greyhound who was tiny but is now irreversibly big (thanks, Dr. Ledarius). These dogs do not shed, but they DO sweat. If you're allergic to dog sweat, we need to see a written note from your doctor explaining how that's possible. (We have never heard of a dog sweat allergy, and are curious.) If you're not allergic, then great!

Because these dogs WILL sweat into your drink.

Parking is simple: we are surrounded on all sides by a huge empty parking lot. Just park there. (Please don't stare at any runes carved into the asphalt.)

For any board game heads out there, we do have copies of some of our faves: Handcrusher; Don't Wake Murderman; Farmquest: Legends of The Barn; Pick-a-Numba!; and Oops, The Blurf Went Away, to name a few.

If anyone does NOT want to play (whaat? no fun!) we may just put you on greyhound duty! (They are a lot of fun but need a lot of love and never sleep. When the board games come out, they scream because they are jealous. You will need to trick them into being quiet. Good luck––the embiggened one has the intelligence of a SMART human.)

Because of the powerful battery-draining electromagnetic field on our block, taking Uber and Lyft is encouraged. We don't want anyone driving home drunk, and Ashley and I own both companies, so we make money on it. Thanks :)

Ashley's Pecan Dindles are extremely intense, so we recommend you only have one. To address a huge problem from our last party: the Dindles are NOT EDIBLE. They are meant to be viewed (NOT edge-on) and appreciated (please!), but you probably should not touch them. Just keep them, ponder them, and do not throw them away—the pecan part is biodegradable (obvi) but the Dindle itself has a half-life of five billion years.

Finally, there is a dress code: clothing! Ha ha. That's just a little joke. The actual dress code is "muppet fur."

That's it! We look forward to seeing you. It feels like forever since the last time we had a thing at our place, and we can't wait to reconnect with all of the survivors. Excited!

CHARLIE HANKIN (@mecharliehankin) *is an L.A.-based cartoonist & writer. His series* **The Summoner** *is now streaming on Peacock. He has contributed cartoons to* **The New Yorker** *since 2013.*

STAG PARTY
BY SIMON RICH
ENDANGERED BEETLE
We recommend 0.0002 mg of Wellbutrin by mouth twice daily, little guy.

According to scientists, climate change has begun to threaten the survival of the stag beetle (lucanus cervus), a family of insects that once thrived in great numbers across Europe. To get a new perspective on the crisis, I interviewed one of them. —SR

SR: What's the best way we can help you guys?
B: Easy. Wipe us off the face of the fucking earth.
SR: So you're saying we've made the environment so terrible, you actually long for death?
B: Oh no, we've wanted out since day one. Our lives are a living hell. Digging through dirt, crawling around. It's a nightmare. When you humans first came on the scene, we looked at each other like, "Thank God, this is it, these guys are gonna step on us and put us out of our fucking misery." Then you do the mammoths, you do the dodos, and we're waiting around, like, "When's our turn?" Still waiting.
SR: If you want to die why do you keep reproducing? I mean, I see you guys mating constantly.
B: That's us trying to kill each other. Every few minutes, we look at each other and psych ourselves up, like, "Come on, let's just fucking *do* each other." And then we charge at each other, really hard, and every time it's like, "Fuck. Worst-case scenario." Then there's three hundred more, and they always say the same thing when they're born: "What the fuck is this shit?" And you have to be like, "Yeah, fuck, I'm sorry, I don't know what to tell you." Step on me.
SR: What?
B: Step on me. Fucking kill me, right now, straight up.
SR: No.
B: Why not?
SR: I'm a journalist. I can't get involved.
B: *Please.*
SR: No.
B: You a Jew?
SR: What?
B: I asked if you're a Jew.
SR: What's that got do with anything?
B: Yes or no?
SR: Yes. I happen to be Jewish.
B: Figures.
SR: What's *that* supposed to mean?
B: I think you know.
SR: Are you trying to antagonize me into stepping on you? Because it's not going to work.
B: Fuck!

latest book is called New Teeth.

GREAT DESIGN BOOKS
By Steven Heller

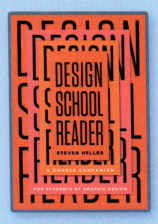

Design School Reader
ISBN: 9781621536901
6" x 9" / 264 pages

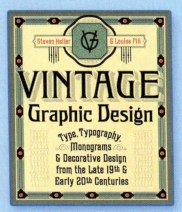

Vintage Graphic Design
ISBN: 9781621537083
8" x 10" / 208 pages

Citizen Designer
ISBN: 9781621536406
6" x 9" / 312 pages

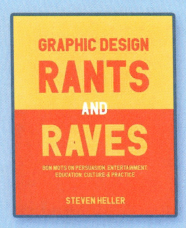

Graphic Design Rants and Raves
ISBN: 9781621535362
7" x 9" / 200 pages

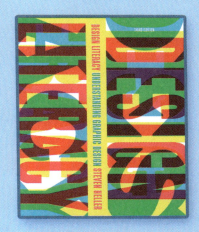

Design Literacy
ISBN: 9781621534044
6" x 9" / 304 pages

Published by Allworth Press in New York City and available from quality booksellers everywhere.

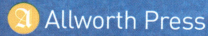

https://www.skyhorsepublishing.com/allworth-press/

NEW FROM FANTAGRAPHICS UNDERGROUND

Coping Skills

HELPFUL DRAWINGS

JOHN CUNEO has drawn *The New Yorker* covers, been featured in *Esquire*, and has won nearly every major illustration award. But many of his drawings are too perverse, neurotic, and untethered for mainstream publication. *Coping Skills* collects a treasure trove of these outré sketches — scenes of domesticated manatees, climate change, and plenty of sex — by one of the finest illustrators working today.

"Complex and hilarious, fearless and shocking, there's no one like Cuneo in the field of illustration today. Perhaps there never was. I laughed out loud several times reading this book. It's hard to stand how drawings imultaneously be so imaginative and so excruciatingly true."
— **David Apatoff**, *Illustration Art*

AVAILABLE NOW AT FANTAGRAPHICS.COM

DREW DERNAVICH

The Tabby.

Tabby Tabby, purring bright,
On the sofa, in the light;
What immortal hand or eye,
Has framed my kitty allergy?

Did God make pets in fine array
And soy and gluten the same day?
Is your fur pollen from grass or tree?
Did he who made peanuts make thee?

Does our creator *meow* commands?
Was it his divine feline plan
To bless you with nine precious lives,
And then to stricken me with hives?

Tell me: in what wicked cauldron
Stirred by demons, or angels fallen
Brew'd your dander which burns my lung?
Swells my nose, and dries my tongue?

Who freed your kind to chase your tails,
While I but wheeze when I inhale?
And gave you *hiss* and *meow* and *mew*
But left me with *ah-choo! ah-choo!*

Why can't I visit friends and neighbors
Unless I impose such labors
Of vaccum, dust, and swiff and mop
So itching in my eyes might stop?

Dost thou know I need HEPA air
To breathe the oxygen we share?
And only dare to sit on rugs
With antihistamines — or drugs?

Yet I surrender my applause
For winsome whiskers, clever paws;
And pray, as I prepare a sneeze:
Can we be friends, not enemies?

Tabby Tabby, purring bright,
On the sofa, in the light;
Tabby, fond of you I am,
But like you more on Instagram.

BRIAN McCONNACHIE

The Lost Mall of Atlanta

Last spring, on the shores of the exclusive Breakers Hotel in Palm Beach, Florida, guests were suddenly confronted with the surreal sight of a shopping mall set right at the water's edge. Its familiar shape and imposing size seemed to banish any concerns of its right to be there, quite the opposite. Instead, witnesses appeared far more delighted than disturbed by this colossal oddity and environmental nightmare suddenly appearing on their fashionable beach. As more of the curious moved closer, the glass doors whipped open and from the roof enormous, red pennants unfurled declaring: EVERYTHING 40% TO 60% OFF.

As accustomed to convenience as many of these vacationers were, they may have assumed this was an extravagant promotional sales stunt which would be to their benefit and so it sent them hurrying off for their wallets and credit cards. When the last of them had entered, the doors slid shut and the immense structure slipped silently back into the calm morning ocean from whence it came.

Friends and relatives of the missing were in disbelief of the eyewitness accounts, and took it upon themselves to hire private detectives to restore their loved ones to them.
But within a month, the detectives were missing as well. The story itself became woefully under-reported and soon entered the foggy realm of urban legend.

Then in early August, at Hilton Head, North Carolina, it happened again. Rising out of the sea like some prehistoric leviathan, the structure slowly drifted towards the shore. Beachgoers who believed themselves to be miles from the nearest retail outlets were bluntly confronted with this unexpected challenge to their disposable income. Some stood waiting at the water's edge holding up their debit cards, while others waded out to meet the marvel halfway, lifting high their fanny packs and shoulder bags. Neither group, for a moment, suspecting that the only bargain they were in for would involve aquatic entombment.

"If I'm not mistaken, it's a whole new breed of shopping mall we're dealing with here," said Robert Coalman, the recently appointed Director of Ambulatory Structures, a division of Homeland Security.

"We believe these malls are proactive, and we're almost certain they have a hostile agenda but we're not exactly sure what that is…beyond luring unsuspecting shoppers through their doors, then drowning them for no plausible reason.

"Every time we try to anticipate the malls' next move," Director Coalman added, "they go ahead and do the exact same thing they did the last time. It has us off-balance.

"It has been speculated that this particular mall is reacting to the dip in consumer confidence and the increases in online shopping. But why would they consume their own consumers is the question."

Is it just rage, pure and simple? But rage about what? What have we done to make them so angry? Is it misdirected rage? Are we going to wake up one morning to a pile of bloated bodies washed up on our shores?

"You have to realize, malls are not that bright," states Coalman. "They're basically right down there with indoor parking garages, storage bins, and FEMA trailers. We're not exactly dealing with buildings like the Chrysler or the Monadnock here."

Brian McConnachie *founded* The American Bystander *in 1981.*

Masters' Photobombs

The rogue mall in question has been identified as The Shops At Villa Rica, a 240,000-sq. ft. structure built during the so-called "Mall Wars," in the western suburbs of Atlanta, Georgia. Malls were being built at such a furious pace, it was inevitable that there would be a serious glut with major fallout. Within three years of its completion, this mall was bankrupt, abandoned, demolished and assigned to landfill.

But it somehow reconstructed itself and made its way down the Altamaha River and into the Gulf of Mexico. There it may have hooked up with one of the smaller but far more rapacious Eastern European malls that have been making their way to our shores, introducing themselves into our rivers and estuaries and have been recently spotted in the Mississippi as far north as St. Louis, Missouri.

A few days following the incident at Hilton Head, a young girl around the age of eight—without any identification and in a bewildered state—was found wandering alone on an empty stretch of beach. She was wearing a 30% cotton 70% polyester blend, pink and white, flame-retardant pajama ensemble, retailing for $14.99...that still had all the tags on it, and was believed to be from the inventory of that same Atlanta rogue mall. Though unwilling (or unable) to speak, the girl continually hummed a version of "My Heart Will Go On" from the popular film *Titanic*. She was brought to Washington, where she was personally interrogated by Director Coalman. Was she put ashore to formally present the grievances of this mall, or all malls in general...but then forgot what she was supposed to say? Or was the mall following a biological imperative, like spawning salmon, trying to find an inland waterway back home and we just haven't noticed this breeding behavior in our buildings? If these malls don't get what they want—presumably what all malls want—higher quarterly sales numbers and a quiet place to breed—what then are they capable of? Have they made any demands? Though it goes without saying that the United States Government does not now, nor will it ever, negotiate with ambulatory retail outlets. Through it all, the child has not spoken a word. Parents? No sign of them.

There is one question that gets to the disturbing heart of it all: if the malls don't get what they want—whatever that is—will they come after us? Will they follow us home? This has been a fear of several past administrations. No President wants it said that on his watch the malls started following the shoppers home like so many disenfranchised panhandlers muttering their contempt for our democratic society, while at the same time enjoying the benefits of running water, muzak, automatic doors and express check-out lines.

As recently as two weeks ago, in the light of a full moon, a number of people witnessed a mall emerge from the Potomac River, cross an interstate and disappear into the tall brush of Rock Creek Park, heading to locations unknown. Perhaps continuing their search for that elusive, inland water route to their sacred breeding grounds.

For the past year and a half, this phenomena appeared to be limited mostly to malls—but that is starting to change. In an act more mischievous than malevolent, the building that houses the Commerce Department seems to have swapped places with the Department of Weights and Measures, though no one seems to be much bothered by this. Indeed, some people who work in the respective buildings have even welcomed the change from their daily routine.

But it grows more serious by the day. People have to get involved and not accept this as the "new normal." We need an urgent defense plan as well as the active support of the American people to make it work.

"We ignore these signs at our peril," warns Director Coalman. "If we don't act now, and in a non-partisan manner—something like a new Manhattan Project..." Director Coalman paused, then ominously quoted the Bible, Ezekiel Chapter 7, verse 13: "...and any building exceeding 600 cubits shall depart its foundation, and bring bloody shame upon its owner. Lies shall spew from their lips and falsehoods shall make the seas unhappy."

...Or will it?

M.K. BROWN

"You're WHAT?"

"Need any help?"

M.K. Brown, *long-time contributor to* **National Lampoon** *and other magazines, author of* **Stranger Than Life**, *is working on a new book about men.* B

OLIVER OTTITSCH

MEANWHILE...IN FEUDAL JAPAN

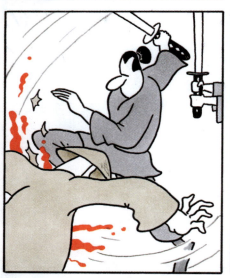

All Clear

These days, you never can tell what somebody else might be thinking.

HAVERSHAM

Banging his large briefcase against the glass as he awkwardly stumbled through the revolving doors, Haversham, who was already having a bad day, entered the enormous marble lobby of the building. As office workers veered around him, he stopped for a moment, looking around to get his bearings and figure out which escalator to take to the upper mezzanine for the meeting. He'd never been here before, so the layout was unfamiliar, and he was nervous about being late to his appointment with the commissioner's assistant at the Municipal Task Force for Gun Violence Solutions. Because of particularly bad crosstown traffic, he was several minutes behind schedule; if that wasn't hassle enough, he'd also forgotten his glasses, so it was difficult to make out the tiny lettering on the card with the room number of the office he was supposed to report to handwritten on the back. As he stood there blinking at the card in his hand, people bustled past, heading in and out of the front entrances; he didn't know anybody who worked in this building, so he paid them no mind. Then he noticed, out of the corner of his eye, a man at the opposite side of the lobby waving a handkerchief.

"Oh, this must be my contact," Haversham thought, waving back with his left hand while putting the card in his inside jacket pocket with his right. He started walking in the man's direction when the man abruptly stopped motioning towards him, turned to the side, and headed off toward the left, ignoring him completely. Haversham was so discombobulated by this strange behavior that it took him a few seconds to figure out what had happened: the man must have mistaken him for someone else, waving him over by mistake. So he stopped walking, pulled the card out of his jacket pocket again, and resumed the task of figuring out where to go. This was an important meeting; must be on time, he needed these people to take him seriously.

It was then that he noticed that the man had stopped walking away and was facing him again, waving. Haversham put the card away and took a few more steps in that direction, but then the man turned and headed away toward the left again—but only got a few steps before swivelling back toward Haversham and waving some more. Haversham, confused, raised his arm a second time, tentatively signalling back, and again, the waving stopped. Haversham hesitated, eyeing the guy with the handkerchief, not at all clear about what the hell was going on.

After a few seconds, the handkerchief started up anew, but as soon as Haversham resumed walking in that direction, the man began to move off, just as before. "Well, do you want me to come over there or not?" thought Haversham, knowing that he was already running late and getting more anxious by the minute. "Make up your mind!" he mumbled irritably, turning his attention to the back of the card a third time—dammit, was that number a four or a nine?—but he could not resist the urge to look back. Sure enough, the man was waving at him again, and again, he stopped. But this time, the enigmatic figure didn't walk away. He just stood there, arms at his sides, looking right at him.

Haversham suddenly experienced an involuntary mental image of an active shooter situation here in the crowded lobby.

There was no doubt about it; this character, whoever he was, was staring directly at his face—everybody else was moving, the two of them were the only ones standing still. There was no one else but Haversham that he could've been looking at. This was too much. Was this guy some kind of a

---

Todd Hanson *worked at* **The Onion** *from 1990 to 2017, and has played TV's Dan Halen on* **Adult Swim's "Squidbillies"** *since 2005.*

a science and could practically do it in his sleep. But Turnblad, who was already having a bad day, still hated having to clean the huge row of floor-to-ceiling glass doors just inside the east entrances to the lobby. They ran the entire length of it, so they took you forever to do; and even after you'd gotten them finished, all day long everyone kept touching them, so you had to go back several times per shift for little spot-checks to polish them up again. Turnblad had done the whole thing from top to bottom before the building opened, so this should only take a few minutes—no need to get the whole squeegee set-up out, a bit of cloth (he always kept one in his back pocket) would do. Still, it was a drag. As he'd done ten thousand times, Turnblad started from the left side and began working his way along the huge wall of glass doors, stopping when necessary to wipe away a patch of streaking or fingerprints before moving on to the next. It was routine and mindless work, and he was only half-paying attention when he noticed, out of the corner of his eye, one of the suits at the other end of the lobby motioning to get his attention.

At first, he thought it was just his imagination, and after a brief pause, Turnblad continued to the right, stopping to wipe off each spot of smudged glass as he went. But no, it wasn't his imagination: a minute later, the guy was signalling him again, this time from closer than before. "What now," thought Turnblad, "somebody else want me to come running and clean up their mess? It never ends."

But this was not one of the people who worked in the building. Turnblad would have recognized him if he was, and the janitorial staff was not used to any of the many visitors, hurrying in and out on official business every day, acknowledging them at all—janitors were mostly invisible to the suits. As Turnblad continued down the line wiping the doors, he saw that the guy was now striding toward him. Why, though, Turnblad couldn't imagine. Did they know know each other from somewhere else? He scrutinized the suit's face carefully but didn't think that they'd ever met. The stranger, squinting, stopped walking forward and just stood there, an odd expression on his

psycho? Come to think of it, he wasn't dressed like a bureaucrat—he was too far away for Haversham to see him clearly, especially without his glasses, but the man appeared to be wearing some sort of a jumpsuit with a light jacket over it, completely inappropriate for an office environment. Did he even belong in this building?

Swallowing his fear, Haversham raised his arm and signalled the man a third time. This time, there was no response—this time, the handkerchief did not wave back. Warily, the two men, about seventy-five feet apart, continued eyeing each other for several increasingly uncomfortable seconds, as the mass of bureaucrats swirled heedlessly around them, entirely unaware of the mounting tension. Now the man, without taking his eyes off Haversham, walked a few more steps to the left, then started waving the handkerchief some more, a bit more vigorously this time, as if impatient. Still staring, Haversham slowly put the card back into his inside jacket pocket.

Suddenly, the strange man dropped the handkerchief to the floor and, with a rapid motion, pulled a small, black object out his jacket. As the man raised it to eye level, Haversham had just enough time to think, "My God, this is really happening," before dropping his briefcase, spinning on his heel, and tearing off toward the escalator like a jackrabbit on fire.

Behind him, he heard a voice shouting "Security! Code red situation!" Only a few seconds had passed; there still hadn't been any shots fired. He had to get clear of the ground floor—the whole open lobby, with all those people crowding in and out, was a target now. Panic electrifying every nerve ending in his body, Haversham raced up the escalator at a full run. By the time he reached the mezzanine, a team of security guards was already there, barrelling toward the crisis from the opposite direction, in emergency-response mode, faces deadly serious.

In that frantic moment he didn't know what to expect, but the last thing in the world Haversham ever thought would occur was—oddly enough—exactly what happened next.

TURNBLAD

He'd been a janitor at various municipal buildings for over twenty years, and at this one for nine—so by this point he had his whole eight-hour shift down to face, peering right at him.

Turnblad suddenly experienced an involuntary mental image of an active shooter situation here in the crowded lobby.

There was no doubt about it: this character, whoever he was, was staring directly at his face—everybody else was moving; the two of them were the only ones standing still. There was no one else but Turnblad that he could've been looking at. This was too much. Trying to look casual, Turnblad walked to the next spot and wiped another smear from the glass. He was getting unnerved. Who was this joker, who evidently had nothing better to do than just loiter in the lobbies of busy buildings, staring at janitors? Didn't he have anywhere he needed to be? Turnblad was sure, now, that he'd never seen this guy in his life. Did he even belong here in the building?

The suit waved at him for the third time. Warily, the two men, about seventy-five feet apart, continued eyeing each other for several increasingly uncomfortable seconds, as the bustling crowd of bureaucrats swirled heedlessly around them, entirely unaware of the mounting tension. Remaining focused on the suit, not daring to take his eyes off him, Turnblad walked to the next spot and wiped the glass again, maybe a little more vigorously than he realized, because the adrenaline was starting to kick in.

Still staring at him, the stranger reached slowly into his inside jacket pocket.

Turnblad dropped the cloth to the floor at his feet and immediately grabbed for the walkie-talkie in his own pocket. Suddenly, the guy threw down his briefcase, pivoted ninety degrees, and started sprinting like a bat of hell towards the escalator to his right.

Turnblad had just enough time to think, "My God, he'll have a line of fire to the whole lobby from up there," before shouting into his walkie-talkie, "Security! Code red situation! Suspect running for north side escalator, heading for the mezzanine!"

By the time the guy reached the top of the escalator, a team of security guards was already there, racing right at him, booking across the mezzanine in the opposite direction. Without hesitation, they tackled the fleeing man at a full sprint, and he went down hard, frantically yelling about a gun. Then someone in the crowd—in a high-pitched, high-volume shriek that was more than enough to set the spines of everyone tingling with terror—started screaming "The briefcase! The briefcase!" More security teams moved in to evacuate the area, which didn't take them very long to do, since by that point everybody had already hightailed it out of there, screaming like banshees and trampling each other in a mad, desperate dash for the exits, as fast as their legs could carry them.

In short order, the suspect, his forehead bleeding from where he'd hit the floor, was hauled out of the building—cursing and struggling, looking dazed from the head injury, and babbling incoherently, "You idiots, the gun's downstairs"—but, because of particularly bad crosstown traffic that day, it was a full twenty minutes before the bomb squad showed up with the robot to open the case he'd dropped in the middle of the vast, now-otherwise-empty, marble floor.

It turned out not to have any explosives inside, thank God—but, in a particularly disturbing development, it was found to contain a lot of suspicious-looking paperwork, obsessively detailing frightening information about public mass-shooting statistics, addressed to the commissioner's assistant at the Municipal Task Force for Gun Violence Solutions. After this was gathered as evidence and turned over to the detectives in charge of the investigation, it was still another two hours, as the police combed every inch of the lobby searching for the missing gun, before the all clear was given for everybody to get back to work.

As he returned to his task of cleaning up the long row of east-entrance inside doors—now smudged beyond belief by the handprints of cops, paramedics, firemen, newspaper reporters, TV crews, fact-finding liaisons from the Mayor's office, emergency trauma-intervention counselors, bomb-removal robot technicians, and hundreds of frantic, screeching, stampeding bureaucrats, thus necessitating a complete floor-to-ceiling redo with the big squeegee rig—Turnblad muttered to himself, "Shit. They should've made this glass bulletproof. These days, you can never tell what somebody might be thinking."

B

"Who's the idiot scientist husband who shrunk us and forgot my birthday NOW?"

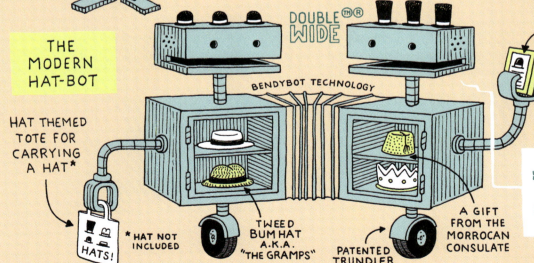

BEN KAWALLER

What I Had Done For Love

For most of my life, I have been blessed with a forgiving metabolism. Until fairly recently, I could stuff my face with relative impunity and still maintain a waistline that gave me a fighting chance at sexually ensnaring people slightly better-looking than I am.

But it seems the party has come to an end.

I first noticed my love handles several months ago when I chanced to take a nude photograph of myself from the back, for my records. The evidence was stark: I am no longer twenty-five.

A little extra padding around the midsection is something most men in their mid-thirties could probably take in stride, but I felt my stock on the dating market had plummeted. I am a gay man living in West Hollywood, and we spend a lot of time shirtless and walking away from each other.

I first tried to attack the problem through dieting. I chose to do the keto plan, which I knew nothing about, except that you ate mostly fat and meat. It felt like a regime I could summon the discipline to stick to, and I took it very seriously, conscientiously stuffing myself with bacon, meatballs, and chicken wings. Several weeks into supposed ketosis, though, my love handles were as fulsome as ever.

Around this time, I was browsing Groupon for a friend's wedding gift when my eye happened to land on a solution I hadn't considered: discount liposuction. Love handles, so this ad for liposuction told me, are notoriously resistant to diet and exercise. It seemed to me, having read this ad for liposuction, that the most appropriate way to deal with my love handles would be to go to what appeared to be a doctor's office and have them physically removed.

Despite my having found him on Groupon, the liposuctionist was a Cedars-Sinai–affiliated surgeon, which eased my fear of quackery. "We'll do your lower back and flanks," Dr. Mohebbi pronounced, appraising my torso. ("Flanks," the technical word for love handles, has to be the rare anatomical term that seems to go out of its way to be hurtful.)

"I can grab more than an inch of fat," he said, his hand full of my pudge. "You make a very good candidate." I was flattered—while also feeling rather like a barnyard animal that would fetch a good price if brought to market.

Leaving the doctor's office, I called my sister to keep her abreast of my plans for my love handles. Zoë is married to a vegetarian and borders on the anemic; needless to say, she always looks fabulous. Zoë was unkind, as she thinks an extra couple of pounds is the least of my problems. "You're pathetic," she said.

"Don't tell Mom and Dad," I said, then rang my brother. Geremy is an older, more stable version of me—gay, but regularly employed. He said, "You're not doing your tummy?"

I called Dr. Mohebbi: "Hey, while you're in there, think you could suck out some from the front?" As it turns out, this was a service the good doctor was willing to let me pay him to provide.

Around this time it occurred to me to Google what the hell liposuction actually is. Here's the skinny: first, they inject your tummy, or "flanks" as the case may be, with a mix of saline, anesthetic, and epinephrine, a capillary restricter that makes the whole thing less bloody. They call this solution a "tumescent," because it causes your body to become hard and swollen. Then the doctor cuts some holes in you and starts ravaging your insides with a tiny vibrating cannula that sucks out your fat cells. After he's done vacuuming your body, he stitches you up, leaving a few open seams so your body can drain out any lingering effluvia. (I would later learn, post-surgery, that it is important to lay down a towel before you sit on the couch.)

The day of my procedure, Dr. Mohebbi had me stand in front of him while he drew circles on my body with black marker—just like on TV! They do this because when they inflate you with the lipo potion you can become asymmetrical, which makes it hard to know where exactly to mutilate you. Gazing at the markings he'd drawn, Dr. Mohebbi was visibly

---

When the world is in session, **Ben Kawaller** *makes funny videos for* **Los Angeles** *magazine and* **Wehoville**. *He has alienated gay Republicans, witches, and men who like to have sex dressed as dogs.*

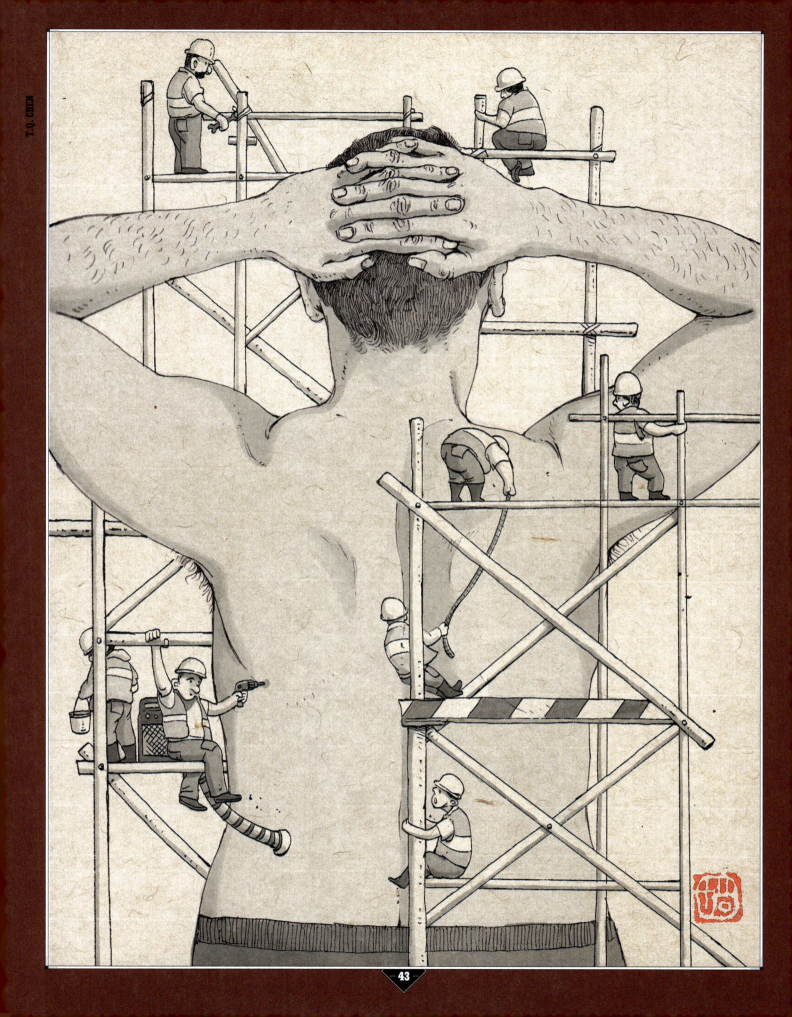

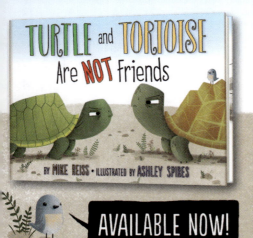

From bestselling author MIKE REISS comes a story of unlikely friendship between two very different animals.

AVAILABLE NOW!

"Humorous and deep."
—KIRKUS REVIEWS

"It becomes clear that some things, from buildings to friendships, just take time."
—PUBLISHERS WEEKLY

"A great addition to any parent, teacher, or librarians' collections."
—CM: CANADIAN REVIEW OF MATERIALS

HARPER
An Imprint of HarperCollinsPublishers
ART © 2019 ASHLEY SPIRES

---

excited. "This is going to look nice!" he said, reinforcing my impression that I was taking the only responsible course of action. And right on cue, the anesthesiologist handed me a consent form and let me know it was possible I might die from this entirely elective, completely cosmetic endeavor. I signed immediately.

Just before I went under the knife, a cheerful nurse approached my bed to inform me that after the surgery I would be sent "a compression garment, which you'll wear 24/7 for twelve weeks."

Wait a second. Possible death was one thing, but this was the first I had heard of any such garment. Did I really have to spend the next three months *in a corset*?

"For the best results, yes. If you want that nice contour," she said, making the shape of a curvaceous woman with her hands. I did indeed want that contour, whatever it was, though I resented Dr. Mohebbi for holding out on me. When we discussed recovery, he'd promised me nothing more than excruciating pain. I considered airing my grievance right then, but thought better of it; you don't want to piss off your doctor moments before he slices you open. And what was I going to do at this point? Walk out of there covered in magic marker, my hideous flanks still intact?

Within five minutes I had drifted off into a fentanyl-induced sleep. When I woke up, I was beautiful.

Well, not quite. The first time I removed my dressings and beheld my new body, I was sure I'd made a terrible mistake. My tummy had a taut, bloated look, as if you could slash me with a knife and I would deflate. Whatever had been done to my "flanks" had left two large mounds on either side of me—my hips seemed to have actually expanded. Evidently, major swelling is a natural result of inflicting bodily trauma by sawing through fatty tissue with a foreign object.

The days following the operation otherwise lived up to Dr. Mohebbi's guarantee: I felt like my abdomen had been assaulted—which it had been. Sadly, the Percocet I'd been prescribed served only to dull the pain, which was so intense the pills didn't even provide a mild buzz. This was unfortunate, as I am sober, and when you're sober, the only highs you're allowed are the ones that are prescribed, so you're constantly looking forward to your next surgical procedure. This was a real letdown. (Fortunately, I have an upcoming root canal.)

For the first forty-eight hours, I was instructed to keep the area iced. Combining One Weird Trick I found online with my own ingenuity, I constructed my own wearable ice packs, which you should definitely try: just pour water and vodka into a few diapers and pop them in the freezer. By velcro-ing two of them together, I made myself a handy iced-diaper belt, which I then strapped

"Keep absolutely still. My husband's vision is based on movement."

WORLD'S HIGHEST FIVE

to my torso, and went about my day. I liked to make extras, adding a little orange juice so that if any guests came by, I could throw them a diaper and have them wring out a few cocktails.

My dreaded compression garment turned out to be sort of a cross between a leotard and a singlet: a sleeveless, thigh-length, Spanx-like thing that hugged me all over, except for a generous open space to allow for personal business. The overall effect was intensely erotic. I didn't want to take it off, even after the garment had gone from a crisp white to a sallow cream, streaked and spattered where I spilled food on it or scratched the scabs on my fat holes.

Even so, it was terrifically flattering. I had corsets all wrong, and for that I'd like to apologize.

In the months since, I am happy to report that the love handles have not grown back (though Geremy assures me they will). But there are other clouds on the horizon: the slowly-encroaching grayness around the temples, the ever-so-slightly marbling skin on the side of my torso, the lines on my forehead. I hope liposuction isn't the first in a long line of cosmetic interventions, all in the service of keeping myself palatable to unforgiving men—a group that, at least for now, includes myself.

In the program I'm in that keeps me sober, they talk of old ideas and new ideas, and I have a feeling that whatever drove me to have my body professionally invaded was an old idea—about myself, and maybe even about men in general. I think most would agree that the sanest course of action going forward is to keep reasonably active, eat reasonably well, let things be what they will be, and hope to fall in love with a person, as opposed to a person's body.

It would be nice to prove capable of such a profound psychic shift. Until then, I will instead do what so many gay men do: try and outrun time, overlook good men with lapsed gym memberships, and endeavor to pair up with another tolerably flawed guy who reluctantly keeps himself better-looking than he should be for the sake of our sex life.

Sometimes I wish I could live up to a loftier ideal than that. But nobody's perfect. **B**

THE VIRTUAL MEMORIES SHOW

In its 8th year, **The Virtual Memories Show** is a weekly podcast hosted by **Gil Roth**, featuring talks with writers, cartoonists, artists, musicians, and other creative types, including these **American Bystander** contributors:

RO Blechman • Barry Blitt • MK Brown
Roz Chast • Seymour Chwast
Joe Ciardiello • John Cuneo
Liza Donnelly • Bob Eckstein
Drew Friedman • Michael Gerber
Mort Gerberg • Sam Gross
Ben Katchor • Ken Krimstein
Peter Kuper • Merrill Markoe
Mimi Pond • Shannon Wheeler

As well as
Jules Feiffer • Ann Telnaes • Moby
Posy Simmonds • Chris Ware
Carol Tyler • Harold Bloom • Ed Ward
Milton Glaser • Molly Crabapple
Pete Bagge • Thomas Dolby • Kaz
Steven Heller • Barbara Nessim
Irvine Welsh, and 300+ more!

"If I've had a better interview, I don't remember it."
—Bruce Jay Friedman • *A Mother's Kisses*

"Gil Roth is a dream interviewer: relaxed, erudite, jaw-droppingly well-prepared, notably gracious in a graceless age."
—Mark Dery • *Born To Be Posthumous*

"He doesn't just ask questions, he wants to know where the answers lead. One of the best interviews I've ever had!"
—Kathe Koja •
Under The Poppy, The Cipher, and *Skin*

"A great, omnivorous interviewer on one of the most entertaining podcasts going."
—Peter Trachtenberg •
Another Insane Devotion

Find The Virtual Memories Show on iTunes & at vmspod.com

Amagola

*It was a good place for drinking.
And for leaving.*

WE WERE in Amagola, like three ticks on a post. The horses were in the livery and we walked to the Silk Hat Saloon. There was nothing for it but to wait for McBride. It was a good place for waiting. The sign above the door read—LIQUOR * BEAUTY * GAMBLING—and was filigreed with bullet holes.

"That's my hole there. In the O," said Lester.

"You had aim then," said Bob.

"Yep," I said.

We passed from the sunlight into the dark, stood at the doorway until our eyes adjusted, then sat at a table. There was nothing for it but to drink. It was a good place for drinking.

Duke, the three-legged dog that lived behind the bar came over to sniff our boots then yawned and walked away, flopped in a corner and attacked his haunches where some burrs had taken up residence. He shook his head as if his ears were full of bees.

"Had a dog named Prince once," said Lester.

"What exactly is a duke?" said Bob.

"What's a baron?" I said.

"We got whiskey here fit for royalty, so what's your pleasure, fellers?" said Spitlock, the barkeep, pimp and proprietor of the Silk Hat, who stood by our table. There was no one else in the place and I guess he came over for the company as much as to sell us some of his liquor.

"Might as well bring a bottle," said Lester.

"That one with the picture of a horse on it," said Bob.

"Bring four glasses and join us," I said.

Bob looked at me funny when I said it. He and Spitlock had a falling-out some years back over a woman who resided upstairs that Bob considered his exclusive squeezer, but who of course needed to make a living, overseen by Spitlock. Bob and the barkeep came to blows. It was a draw, and anyway she left town with a banker from Wheatstraw. But grudges were one of the few forms of entertainment available at no cost around here, so Bob and Spitlock made a half-hearted play at it.

"Yeah, why not," they each said at the same time and we all laughed and Duke looked up at the sound.

We sat around exchanging lies and emptying the bottle, then another, rolling smokes and nodding off in our chairs until the sun started down and some other folks came in for their evening slurp; farmers and cowboys and shopkeepers from town, a tin horn who shuffled a deck of cards at another table. A couple of girls came down from upstairs, scratching and yawning and trying to smile at the men who'd seen those smiles a hundred times before. Spitlock was back behind the bar. He had a pet crow named Morgan who walked along the bar picking up anything shiny then flying off with it. He stole a lot of coins this way and Spitlock claimed no responsibility for the losses—but did manage to find the bird's hidey-hole one time and bought himself a new hat.

The crow flew out the door with a

Lou Beach *is a writer and artist living in Los Angeles.*

silver dollar in its beak just as McBride walked in.

He stood in the doorway silhouetted by the setting sun. When he laid eyes on us, he reached for his gun and me and Bob and Lester drew our shooters and shot him dead before he could fire. Duke whimpered and slinked off behind the bar. Spitlock came out and removed his apron and spun it through the air to rid the place of all the gun smoke.

"Well, hell," he said, nudging McBride with his boot.

"I got him in the neck," said Lester.

"It was a clean shot," said Bob.

"Yep," I said.

We threw some money on the table and walked out of the Silk Hat and got our horses from the livery. There was nothing for it but to leave Amagola. It was a good town for leaving.

EDDIE CAMPBELL

"Your Aunt Kate"

As the Twentieth Century dawned, one beloved cartoonist introduced millions of readers to Picasso, Marconi, and a panoply of doomed aviators.

Let me tell you about Kate Carew. She was probably America's first great woman cartoonist. But whether or not that is worth debating (other female artists were amusing before her), it would be more useful to simply say that her story is uncommonly fascinating. And she was a funny lady.

Kate Carew was not her real name. She had three successive married names while she was Kate Carew. It existed in fiction before she adopted it, but we will not dally with that here. Nor with the fact that it was elsewhere given to a chestnut filly.

Kate's career took her from San Francisco to London and Paris and back, six times by my count, an impressive record for the opening years of the 20th century. Pulitzer's *New York World*—and the "yellow journalism" for which it was famous—was at its zenith when Kate first appeared there in 1900. She showed up in the wee hours after attending the theater, her witty observations about the performance recorded in both words and pen sketches. Unusual as such a presentation was, *The World*'s city editor went for it, and so did readers. After that, they couldn't get enough of Kate Carew.

In one of my favorite examples of Kate's theatrical reviewing, she wrote about the sparseness of a production of *Romeo and Juliet*, in which scenes were indicated by placards instead of realistic scenery: "'A Street,' 'A Garden,' rather than by 'property trees, and furniture by So-and-So (with a notice in the programme)," she wrote. The critics didn't like the innovation—"They loosed shafts at Capulet's rough-house balcony"—but Kate disagreed; the idea fit well with her cartoonist's embrace of nonliteralness: "Stage illusions don't illooze. If they did—if [Broadway impresario David] Belasco could make you forget that you were in a theatre and believe that you were watching actual occurrences in Japan and Purgatory and Heaven—you would be a logical candidate for a keeper and a straitjacket. Which leads up to this—that *Romeo and Juliet* in the interesting Elizabethan fake at Mrs. Osborn's, without scenery or effects, came as near to illoozing me as any stage spectacle I ever saw—infinitely more so than Mansfield's 'steenty-billion-dollar *Brutus*. Some of the Elizabethans are quaint actors. Popper Capulet outcherries the Cherry Sisters*, but Harry Leighton's Mercutio is like a generous act in a pawn office."

Kate's quiver of verbal projectiles included playful misspellings, invented words, mock accents and urbane wit, putting her at the pointy end of American journalistic wiseassery. This style fit perfectly with her art, as you can see by the funny drawing on page 51, of Romeo calling to his beloved Juliet on the non-existent balcony,

Kate wrote and drew, both, which was the unusual part of it. She wrote the theater review, and on Sundays the celebrity interview, and made caricatures and incidental sketches to accompany each. She was equally adept at these normally separate jobs—but instead of drawing attention to her skill, Kate had a disarming way of referring to herself in her pieces variously as "a mere scribbler person," also "a mere sketcher" depending on her role in the exact moment. She presented herself humbly as "your Aunt Kate," and addressed her readers as "dears." Carew's complete package took a while to coalesce of course, but by the time it was ripe, she had 👉

(* The Cherry sisters' vaudeville act was so bad that it had to be seen to be believed, guaranteeing them a long career.)

◆

Eddie Campbell *has been drawing comics for four decades. He was the artist on the Alan Moore-scripted* **From Hell.** *The autobiographical is his preferred mode, as you can see in that grand retrospective,* **Alec: The Years Have Pants***. It was while investigating the artist as self-chronicler that he developed something of a crush on the self-chronicling Kate Carew.*

added a very engaging cartoon version of "Aunt Kate" to the proceedings. And this for me is the loveliest part of it.

The bespectacled "Aunt Kate," in her enormous black hat, was usually depicted conducting the interview, perched behind her sketch pad, as in the one at right with the great sculptor Auguste Rodin, monumental like his Thinker. But sometimes in the drawings she is also up and about in the world, as below when we see her landed on the dock at Le Havre, France, in the miserable rain, with three boys helpfully lugging her baggage.

On another occasion, in an example of stunt journalism unworthy of celebration except as a piece of glorious nonsense, she passed herself off as a millionaire in order to be the first guest to sleep in the ten-thousand-dollar bed (about $290,000 in today's money), at the brand new St. Regis hotel in Manhattan. It was an antique of pre-revolutionary France, and Kate imagined aristocrats in it, prior to their beheadings. "It has all been skillfully arranged in advance. I am expected. I have even been registered. Nobody knows that I am a scribbler person. Nobody knows anything about me except that I am acceptably accredited and have decided to become the first occupant of the Royal suite—for a night and a day I'll be a millionairess—and dash the expense!" The *Sunday World* gave it a huge double-page spread in four colors; Kate rose to the occasion with a long account of her undercover success, adorned with five large composed pictures, two freestanding figures, a copy of the dinner bill, and a photo of the bed (which might tend to suggest some collusion with the establishment... but let's not allow that to spoil a good story). The picture on page 52 shows Kate arriving to dinner, dressed up in cartoon mauves, with an entourage, one

NEW-YORK TRIBUNE, SUNDAY, OCTOBER 13, 1912.

ut Parisian Ways Reveals Rodin

"WHY SHOULD I GIVE UP MY WORK JUST AS I AM CROWNING MY LIFE'S TOIL!"

FOR THE MOMENT I WISHED I WERE BACK ON THAT DEAR OLD BROADWAY.

"Aunt Kate" considers the famous sculptor, 1912.

of whom is recognizable as her then real-life husband, Harrie Chambers. But of course, "Aunt Kate" is not married. Don't tell anyone.

Then there are the celebrity interviews: while many of Kate's approximately 250 subjects are now forgotten, there were a surprising number of outsized individuals whose shadows are cast all the way down to our own time. Her first subject was Mark Twain; her last, Pablo Picasso.

For the most part she caught her celebrities at the time they were doing the thing that they would be famous for, and not years later when they were on the talk show circuit to promote the memoir. Boxer Jack Johnson was the heavyweight champion of the world when Kate caught up with him. Christabel Pankhurst, the famous suffragette, had the police looking for her all over Britain when Kate talked with her in Paris. As Kate wrote, Pankhurst was "very sunburned and had a color that made every woman within sight look a chalky pallor. Her eyes seemed bluer and brighter than any I had seen for weeks, and altogether she was the image of a slender, healthy, happy schoolgirl out for a holiday. You wouldn't believe she was a hardened criminal, a suffragette Joan of Arc, leader of a hundred gallant charges against the London police."

Aunt Kate's timing was impeccable: she

interviewed Picasso the month of the opening of the Armory Show. And she spoke to radio pioneer Gugliemo Marconi a week before the disaster of the *Titanic*, of which Britain's postmaster-general said, "Those who have been saved, have been saved through one man: Mr. Marconi, and his marvelous invention."

There was a spell that seemed perhaps too long when her editor sent her to talk to a series of politicians—"the grand panjandrums of state," as she called them. There were lady writers and actresses, and many figures who were not really celebrities but were people in interesting positions, such as the man in charge of issuing marriage licences at City Hall. Kate usually arrived at the interviewee's abode or office in a horse-drawn cab of the era, whose variety intrigues us at this remove: "I climbed into a fly"..."I hiked myself into an antediluvian hansom"..."I lolled back in a fiacre and rolled along, studying the Eiffel Tower in profile." She imagined herself flying a little plane to interview the accomplished flyer, John Moisant.

Aviators were the heroes of the age, and Kate had a fascination for them. In speaking with them, she nicely caught the uncertainties of the brave new century. A month after their interview, "King of Aviators" John Moisant died in a preparatory flight for his attempt to win the Michelin Cup. The first lady aviator, the vivacious Harriet Quimby, plunged to her death from a thousand feet in Boston, five weeks after her published conversation with Kate. The celebrated balloonist Alberto Santos-Dumont was only spotted briefly enough to catch a likeness: "M. Santos-Dumont was pointed out to me yesterday as he hurried along the Champs-Élysées, twirling his cane and apparently lost in a daydream of aerial adventure. All Paris is looking forward to the plucky little Brazilian's next balloon trip."

Carew's take on the scenery-less Romeo and Juliet, *an illusion that almost—but not quite—illoozed.*

"Aunt Kate," husband secretly by her side, goes into dinner at the St. Regis. Later, she would sleep in a $10,000 bed.

One of her questions to the Wright brothers, builders and flyers of the first successful airplane, was farsighted in the way that only naive questions can sometimes be:

"'Will they ever be used for transporting large numbers of people as railroads are?' I asked.

'No,' said Wilbur, 'that would be too expensive.'

'Or for carrying freight?'

'They could be used for first-class mail,' put in Orville, hopefully."

A couple of years back, after landing in San Francisco and being sped a ways up the California coast, I spent a day with Kate Carew's papers. Kate was a newspaper person who typically believed herself to be only as good as her next story, with all the older ones used to wrap fish, make *papier mâché* or line cat-litter boxes. The collection of copies of her work has a functional look, of something being kept only for her reference rather than as an archive for the ages. A couple of her cartoons have phone numbers and sums she pencilled on them, the only blank space to hand when she was between here and there.

I felt like I was enjoying the company of a sibling of the pen among these assorted tearsheets, uncarefully scissored photos, and even some some recently framed originals. My wife, Audrey Niffenegger, and I were calling ourselves the "digital art burglars." We had a small portable-but-high-quality scanner and the tools necessary to unframe a picture and then reframe it exactly as we found it (this being one of Audrey's many skills). I was gathering material for a book about Aunt Kate, and we two spent some happy hours mining the mother lode.

Kate Carew had a twenty-five year career in the papers. It ended in 1920, due to the kind of eye problems that can arrive after close graphic work produced to deadline over and over for years. She then painted, was accepted to exibit in the Paris Salon three times. Then Kate Carew lived, contentedly, for forty years after her last illustrated article.

Christine Chambers was fifteen years old when her grandmother Mary Williams—the woman who once signed her work "Kate Carew"—died in 1961. Christine knew of the paintings, because they were hanging around the place when she was growing up, but Grandma mustn't have talked much about the other stuff.

Christine didn't know until she was in her forties that Grandma once wielded a famous pencil in the yellow journals of Pulitzer and Hearst, among many other papers and magazines. Since arriving at this knowledge, back in the '90s, she has done a great deal to preserve Kate Carew's name and work and her uncommonly fascinating story. The funniest part of the story, I keep thinking, is one day discovering that your Grandma was in a room with Sandwina the human Hercules. And Picasso and Gertrude Stein in Paris. And was near enough to a young Winston Churchill at a ball in London to sketch him treading on a lady's gown. Not to mention that ten-thousand-dollar bed.

R.O. BLECHMAN

HEAVENLY PASSAGES

Wilson Molde often visited the All Saints Cemetery in the Hamptons,...

...The final resting place for some of America's finest writers:
Beatrice Plumb:
"A Woman in Spite of it All"
"Men, & Other Complaints"

Sylvia Satinwood:
"Craven Hall"
"Craven Hall Revisited"
"Return to Craven Hall"

Calvin Kane:
"Shrike"
"Shreik"
"*#†*!!@"

Molde would draw inspiration from the illustrious surroundings.

...and may his soul rest in Eternal Peace.

BEATRICE PLUMB!? — I Am. And you are...? — I'm Wilson Molde. — I don't recognize the name. — CALVIN KANE! I've read all your books! — Of course. And whom am I addressing? — Wilson Molde. I just wrote a book. — Indeed!

Soon Molde encountered many of the famous residents.

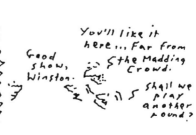

The floodgates have opened. — Next they'll let in JOURNALISTS! Dante's lowest level. — Alright, I'll leave... I suppose. — But we could use a fourth for Bridge. — Good show, Winston. — You'll like it here... Far from the Madding Crowd. Shall we play another round?

Over 140 posters by **Seymour Chwast** created in a period of more than 6 decades with an introduction by **Shepard Fairey** and foreward by **Steven Heller**.

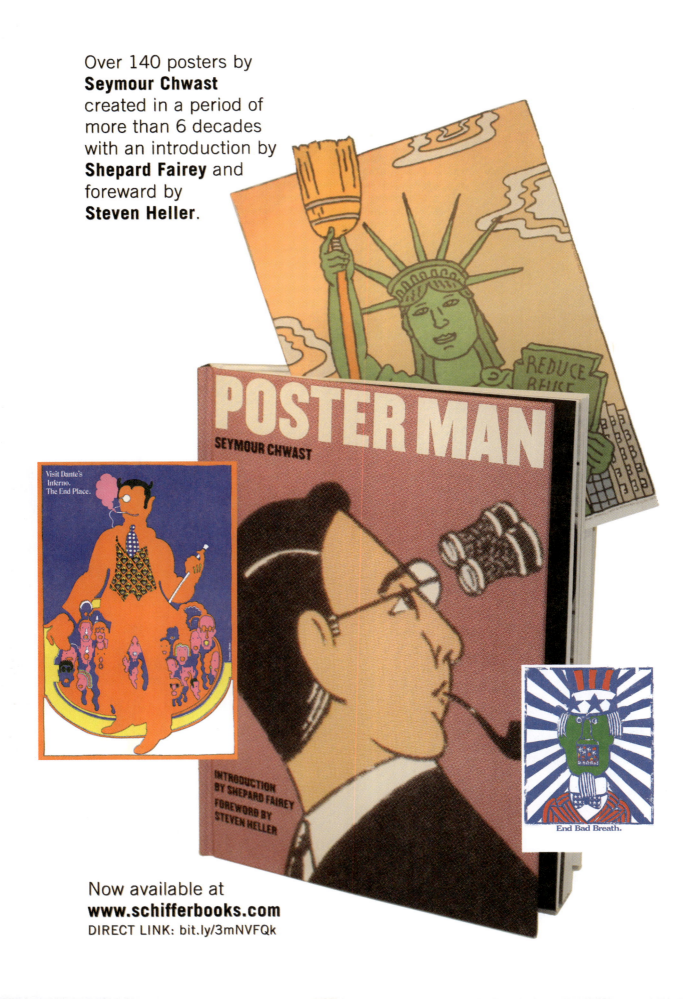

Now available at
www.schifferbooks.com
DIRECT LINK: bit.ly/3mNVFQk

RICH SPARKS

Chicago-based **Rich Sparks** has drawn for The New Yorker, WSJ, Barron's and many other publications. He is also a member of the power pop quintet The Last Afternoons.

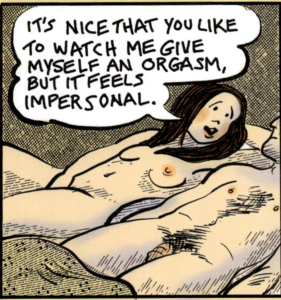

ALAN GOLDBERG

Saturdays

I spent a lot of time with my father before I was a teenager. Saturdays, I sat in his office while he worked. Sundays, I took him to the parts of the city that interested me, usually those tied to transportation. Train stations, airports, air terminals, even bus terminals—the whiff of escape must have pulled at me almost as powerfully as the sweet sense of safety I felt with my father.

It was in the Saturdays at the office, just the two of us there, that we were closest, though we spoke little all day. I don't know what my father felt about these visits. I trusted he enjoyed my company, but he was there to get work done, and he did it.

As he worked through his bills and bookkeeping on one side of the office, I made little plastic models on the other. His company and his office were both small. It had no interior walls because he wanted to know what everyone was doing at all times. He was a self-made man, possessing all the impatience with his employees that goes with assuming he still knew well enough to do it all himself, as he once had. But my father liked what he did, and was good at it, and my sense of his strength no doubt arose from that.

Like so much of New York at that time—the early 1950s—my father was a man who ran to grays and browns. His office followed suit: standard-issue furniture, old-fashioned adding machines and typewriters, brown walls, brown shelves, brown desks. He preached honest work and, though he took pleasure in fixing things and in the promise of any gadget he could find on Canal Street, décor was a notion as foreign to him as it was natural to my mother. This office was him.

Who else would have allowed himself to be talked into a two-toned red and white car…and then had it repainted gunmetal grey? It was one of the geologic faults on which his relationship with my mother lay: She loved the things that being the wife of a successful businessman could buy, whereas he felt the world would be no poorer if the entire contents of Tiffany's were dropped into the Hudson.

Though silence was never demanded on these Saturdays, it was the quiet working near each other that was so reassuring to me, at a time when anxiety seemed to permeate everything I did, every thought I had. My father had vanquished his own anxiety, I realized later, by living life as if it was a permanent condition. He had, over the years, refined his life into a small number of unchanging routines, including this one.

And the ritual reached its high point at lunch. I adored hamburgers, and had two or three favorite spots around the city; the best, by far, was a small place called Broadway Burger at 27th and Broadway, a couple of blocks south of the office that, like so many such places, had a mix of pleasant efficiency and easy laughter. It was a place designed to serve the working man, and it made me feel like one, too.

I'd bring the burgers back, always done up the same way, and my father and I would sit and eat them at a table covered with phonebooks and billing orders. Always, I would start our conversations as if I was a work associate there for a business lunch. "How's business?" I'd ask.

And I can't remember one thing about our conversations after that. It was as if they were just the mumblings of a conversation overheard. The fact of words spoken and the normalcy of two men in lunchtime conversation was the point; it was so comforting that it thrilled me. We'd munch happily for a half hour or so and get back to work.

One Saturday, otherwise normal, I headed to Broadway Burger. Within a block, the smell of drenched ash was in the air, and, when I got there, the place was gone, fresh plywood over the windows, black streaks up and down the white stucco, piles of water-soaked debris in the gutter. Though Broadway continued about its business around me, I was absolutely alone. I felt betrayed by this wreck in front of me; it was as if it had become a central point in my life only to teach me to count on nothing.

In disbelief, I returned to the office. "Oh yeah," my father said, as if he'd just neglected to tell me a friend had called, "I forgot to tell you. It burned down on Wednesday."

I realized at once that my father's experience of these Saturdays was very different from mine. I had called on him to serve as an ally against an almost metaphysical inner turmoil, but for him our quiet companionship was only that.

I could not express at that age what I felt. I could hardly express it to myself. But the Saturday visits ended soon after that day.

B

Alan Goldberg *is Senior Editor of this magazine.*

NICK SPOONER

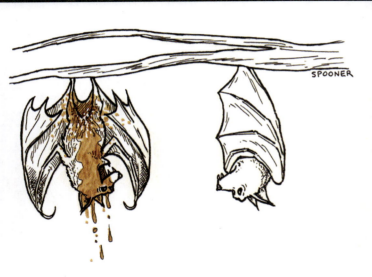

"I like Mexican, but Mexican sure don't like me."

PIÑAUGHTY

VAMPIRE FRAT

"All right you guys, what's so goddamn funny?"

Nick Spooner *is a commercial film director who dreams of becoming a full-time cartoonist.*

MERRILL MARKOE

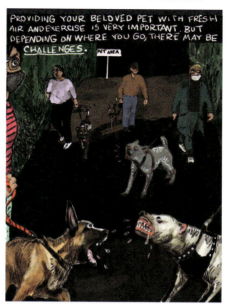

"HUGE FAN!"

Elvis is Alive and Well
inside these pages

Seymour Chwast
Steven Brower

Contents

Introduction
In the Beginning
Sun Records
Musical Influences
First Records
Col. Parker
Jackie Gleason
Milton Berle
Ed Sullivan
In the Army
Graceland
Viva Las Vegas
Frank Sinatra
Concerts
Pink Cadillac
Poster
Women (and One Man) Who Dated Elvis
Masculine Idols / Heroes
Films
Comeback
The Beatles
Elvis Meets Nixon
What He Wore
Hair
Guitars
Songs
Tours
Priscilla
Divorce / Drugs
Final Days
Filmography
Albums
Singles
The Critics
Elvis Speaks
What He Ate
Bibliography

www.yoebooks.com

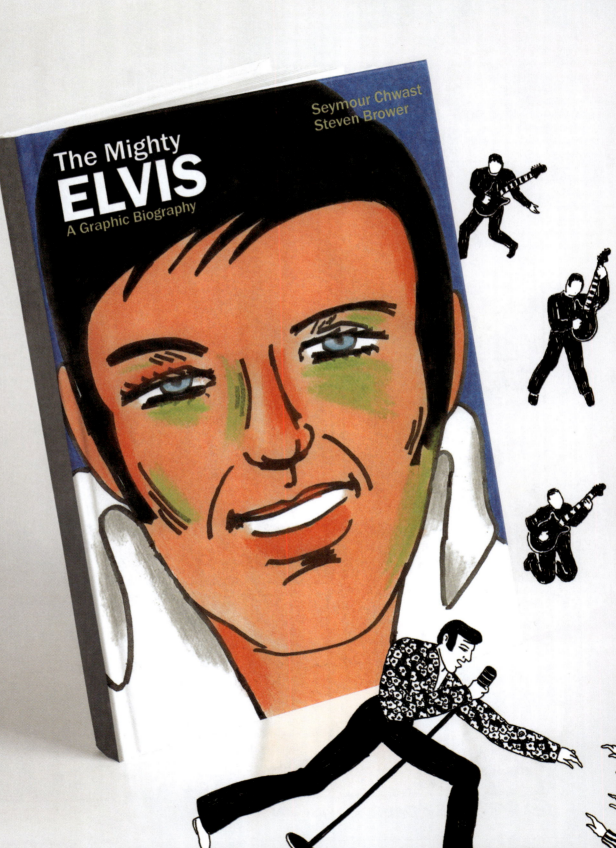

RON BARRETT'S ART MART

They hung my possums upside down in The Louvre.

From the beloved children's book, *Animals should definitely not wear clothing*

You can hang them right side up in your home.

Or choose from any of these other attired animals

Nice prints $250 each, signed to a person of your choice.
Direct from Ron Barrett barrettuws@gmail.com to your walls.

OUR BACK PAGES

NOTES FROM A SMALL PLANET
Any halfway-decent phrenologist would have a field day with Keith • By Rick Geary

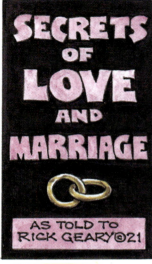
SECRETS OF LOVE AND MARRIAGE
AS TOLD TO RICK GEARY ©21

I GREW UP A SIMPLE FARM GIRL.

SO HOW DID I END UP MARRIED TO KEITH?

HE WAS SO HANDSOME AND DYNAMIC, THE ENVY OF ALL.

AT ANY GATHERING MEN AND LADIES FLOCKED AROUND HIM.

WHILE I SHRANK INTO A CORNER, A DRAB LITTLE WALLFLOWER.

SO I DECIDED UPON A TOTAL MAKEOVER: HAIR, MAKEUP AND FASHION!

AS A PROUD NEW WOMAN, I HURRIED HOME TO KEITH.

BUT I FOUND THAT HE HAD BEEN ARRESTED FOR SECURITIES FRAUD.

HE'S NOW IN THE FEDERAL PEN FOR A LENGTHY TERM.

WHAT COULD I DO BUT RETURN TO THE FARM?

SOMEHOW, LIFE ISN'T THE SAME.

Champagne, Popsicles, LSD and Pringles? Yes please, it's party time!

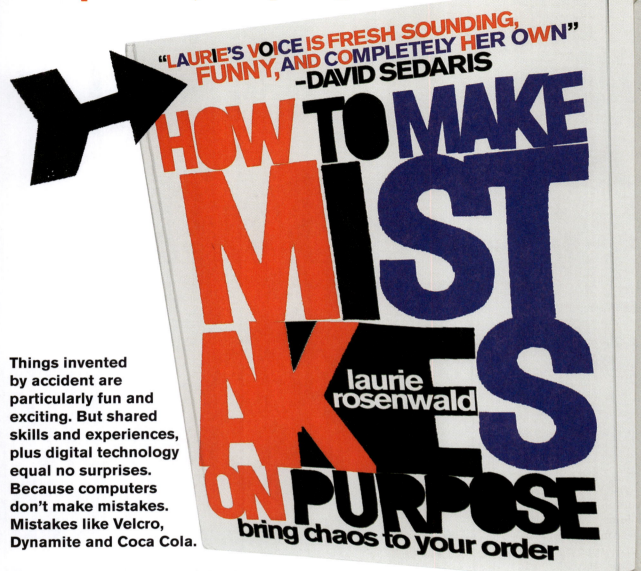

Things invented by accident are particularly fun and exciting. But shared skills and experiences, plus digital technology equal no surprises. Because computers don't make mistakes. Mistakes like Velcro, Dynamite and Coca Cola.

From **AMERICAN BYSTANDER** contributor and author of "All the Wrong People Have Self Esteem" comes the only book you and your family will ever need: HOW TO MAKE MISTAKES ON PURPOSE.

When you surprise yourself, you surprise others. And that is priceless in a world where everything seems to have been done.

INCLUDES:
Your Pointless Quest for Perfection
There's a Nipple in My Room!
Mindfulness Causes Angst, or Why P.G. Wodehouse is my Therapist
That's Not the Rashomon I Remember!
Too Late to Die Young Now

Available Wherever Books are Sold.

Because Trying to be Creative Works About as Well as Trying to be Charming

OUR BACK PAGES

WHAT AM I DOING HERE?

Welcome to the wettest country this side of Atlantis • By Mike Reiss

How to Beat the High Costa Rica

To all my friends who told me to visit Costa Rica—you are no longer my friends.

From the dawn of time until 1986, few people lived in Costa Rica and nobody visited. Then, in 1987, it became a hub of ecotourism; to give you a taste of those times, that same year, the #1 movie star on earth was Steve Guttenberg. Today, more than a million Americans visit Costa Rica every year—a million *and two*, counting me and the wife. The locals are warm and friendly—in fact, a little too warm and friendly for the Covid Age. It's a nation of loud, laughing close-talkers. All the hotels and restaurants are just lovely.

But make no mistake—it's a jungle out there.

And what is a jungle but ferns growing on trees, vines growing on ferns, and moss growing on vines. It's a dark, dense chaos of green and it all looks the same: a five-mile hike in the north looks just like five one-mile hikes in the south. Werner Herzog, who made so many films set in the jungle, put it best: "Nature here is violent. I would see fornication, and asphyxiation, and choking. And fighting for survival, and growing, and just rotting away." In case you didn't get the point, he added, with typical German light-heartedness, "The trees here are in misery. The birds are in misery. I don't think they sing, they just screech in pain."

This is what you go to Costa Rica to see. There are five hundred thousand different animal species in the country, but they all live in a jungle, with infinite places to hide. We hired a tracker to help us find them—his name was Diego, and he looked exactly like our driver who looked exactly like our hotel clerk, and they all looked just like Josh Gad. Because it is a small, closely-knit country, there's much less diversity among the people than the parrots. There are basically four different faces shared by all of Costa Rica's men (and a few of its women): everyone looks like Josh Gad, Ed Asner, Mario Lopez or Patton Oswalt. While that's an amazing cast for a sitcom, it's weird for a whole country. If Patton ever robs a bank here, there will be at least one million suspects.

Diego, our tracker, led us through the jungle promising we might see monkeys and pumas and tapirs, oh my! For two hours, we saw nothing. Suddenly Diego froze in his tracks.
DIEGO: Look! Up in the tree!
ME: Which tree? Your entire country is a forest.
DIEGO: In the *Soncoya* tree, behind the *Pitanga* tree behind the *Palanga* tree. Sixty feet up—it's a sloth!
ME: I couldn't see that if I was Superman.

Diego handed me some binoculars, and I finally made out a curled-up furry ball hanging from a branch. To me, it looked like the tree's testicle. To my wife, it was ADORABLE. Mind you, from a distance of four hundred yards, anything looks adorable. A hospital dumpster. A burning schoolbus.

So the day wasn't a total loss, Diego trained his telescope on the top of another tree so we could see actual wildlife: a wild avocado. Holy guacamole.

We later learned there were many other things in that jungle we couldn't see: poisonous snakes, scorpions, tarantulas, and a tiny tree frog with enough venom to kill a thousand people. Who thought that was necessary? Who figured a bite-size frog could have so many enemies? Even smaller and harder to avoid were the army ants. They lock onto you with their poison pincers, then send out a pheromone message to their billion brothers: "Hey get over here and let's eat this guy!"

It's not just the little things you can't see in Costa Rica—there are big things too, like a volcano. Mount Arenal is one of the natural wonders in the country, but it's perpetually blanketed in fog. Diego raved about it:
DIEGO: When the sky is clear, you can see the volcano for forty kilometers in every direction.
ME: Is it beautiful?
DIEGO: I don't know. I've never seen it.

He then added, somewhat unnecessarily, "You couldn't see it even before Covid."

It made you wonder if there was even a volcano there at all. Perhaps a couple of entrepreneurs collected all the fog machines from Costa Rica's bankrupt discos and piled them up in one place. They had created a permanent cloud bank, but what could they do with it?
ENTREPRENEUR #1: We could tell people there's a mountain under it.
ENTREPRENEUR #2: Too boring.
ENT. #1: How about a dragon?
ENT. #2: Too crazy.
ENT. #1: How about a volcano?
ENT. #2: Bueno! That's like a mountain version of a dragon.

A second tour guide, also named Diego, also resembling Josh Gad, led us on another hike. It was three hours straight up a muddy mountain, to see Mistico, "the river with blue water."

"But Mike," you may be asking, "isn't all water blue?"

YES!!!!!

For the entire hike, Diego 2 berated me for the things I didn't bring:
"You no bring mosquito repellent?"
"You no bring binoculars?"

MIKE REISS is Intrepid Traveler for *The American Bystander*.

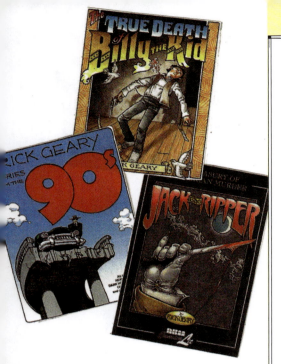

BOOKS & POSTCARDS by RICK GEARY

VISIT THE STORE AT
www.rickgeary.com

HOME TOWN PRESS
Carrizozo NM

"You no bring hiking boots?"
"You no bring lunch?"
"You no bring horsefly spray?"

First of all, is that even a thing? Second, as a tour guide maybe he could have told me what to bring IN ADVANCE. Of course, if I had, I'd be lugging about two hundred pounds of stuff straight up a mountain.

We reached the summit, which would have been a perfect spot to see "the river with the blue water," except the valley was covered in fog. So *Diego Dos*, as the locals would call him, began a lengthy lecture on the difference between moss and lichen. All at once, the clouds opened up with a rainstorm of Biblical proportions. Diego 2 ignored it, continuing on with this lecture nobody asked for. The one thing he never said to me? "You no bring umbrella?" because Costa Ricans aren't bothered by rain. They, like fish, are not actually aware they're wet. Diego 2 finished his speech, and noticed I was now drenched to the skin. He said, "Man, you sure sweat a lot."

This is an important fact nobody tells you about Costa Rica: *it never stops raining*. Sometimes it's a drizzle, sometimes a downpour, and there's a once-in-a-century flood twice every week. The only wetter country on Earth is Atlantis.

It's called a tropical rain forest, but it should be called a rainy tropical rain forest where it rains all the goddam time. This is why you never see the wildlife: every animal knows to go for cover when it rains. Every animal, that is, except the Costa Rican tourist: *Boobus Costa Ricus*.

"I thought this was the dry season!" I raged at one of the Diegos.

"Yes. We get a lot of rain during the dry season."

"Well, when do you get the least rain?"

"During the rainy season."

Besides the rain forest, Costa Rica has a cloud forest, because all their forests have bad weather. There's also a tropical dry forest, but my guide assured me, "It rains a lot there."

My wife and I got back to the hotel that night and hung all our wet clothes out to dry. The next morning, we were surprised to learn that our wet clothes were even wetter. And they stank.

"You stink," my wife told me.

"You stink," I replied. It was like a grade school production of *Who's Afraid of Virginia Woolf?*

The damp had permeated everything. Our dry clothes were now wet. Money turned to mush. Envelopes sealed themselves. Extra Crunchy Cheetos became regular Cheetos.

I tried going out in a rain poncho, but hiking in the tropics while sealed into non-breathable plastic tends to cook one alive. I actually smelled like the Swanson's Boil-in-Bag Chicken A La King Dinners my mother slowly poisoned me with as a child. (Nowadays they call this cooking *sous vide* and charge eighty bucks a plate for it.)

So that was my vacation—two weeks slogging through the jungle in pouring rain, seeing less wildlife than I do on an average New York subway ride. Rats are wildlife, right?

I hated Costa Rica. So why do millions of Americans say they love it?

Maybe they hate to admit they spent precious time, and even more precious money, on a trip they didn't like. I don't have that problem. I'm willing to say things no one else will: *Ghostbusters* isn't funny; *Mad Men* is boring; chocolate lava cake is not worth the wait. My motto is, "If you don't have something bad to say, don't say anything at all."

Or maybe it's Wayne Newton Syndrome. I've been told that Wayne Newton was a masterful entertainer in his time. In my time, he's kind of sucked, doing a lousy Vegas show for decades. Audiences walk out disappointed but saying, "I heard he was good last night." Maybe Costa Rica is the Wayne Newton of Central American countries; you get rained on for a week, but tell yourself, "I heard it was sunny last week."

Even I will admit there are some nice things about Costa Rica:

The hot springs of Tabacon. A dozen warm-water pools, each one unique; a perfect blending of nature and design.

Drinking water is free in restaurants, something you don't find anywhere outside the US.

You'll see six or seven rainbows every day.

Basically, if there's anything good about having way too much water, you'll find it in Costa Rica. And I've been told the country's Nicoya Peninsula is warm and dry. But Mel Gibson lives there, so, ick.

OUR BACK PAGES
DAYBREAK AND A CANDLE-END
In which a flounder is used as a Moleskine • By Ron Barrett

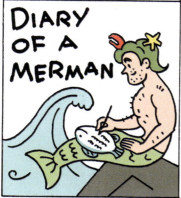

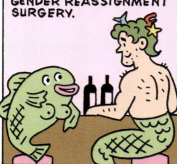
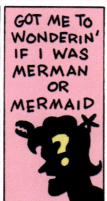

OUR BACK PAGES

ROZ'S MARVELOUS COLLAGES
Japanese matchbox covers from anonymous artists, 1920–40. I need a haircut. • By Roz Chast

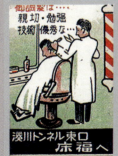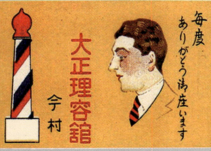

OUR BACK PAGES

P.S. MUELLER THINKS LIKE THIS
The cartoonist/broadcaster/writer is always walking around, looking at stuff • By P.S. Mueller

Chicken Resurrection Day

House cats began to disappear. Some old lady on Cedar Street dragged a mangled cock-a-poo all the way into the mud room, but it was too late for them both. Angry beaks were waving outside. A large noise like a billlion castanets chattered in from the east, getting closer. It was CHICKEN RESURRECTION DAY, and revenge was in the air. A broken pecking sound rose up as trillions, yes, *trillions* of wingless chickens stormed across the land, especially Indiana.

They had been plucked pink by New Jersey marines. They were sunburned and leathery—vicious living jerky. Roasters with razor beaks and no wings, and they meant to flay us all.

That's when the pets started going missing. When the little ones out in their yards began to disappear, it got weird. Spindly old people stopping to check heart rates on daily walks were left behind like little piles of Honduran coffee grounds. A featherless horde, their useless wings revoked, advanced like, well, a legion of clumsy naked chickens.

The birds, if you still call them birds, went on a massive clack attack and headed across Ohio and Indiana, shredding every plant and creature along their murderous way...until a shuddering roar rolled up and down the landscape, crumpling silos, feed lots, loafing pens, everything.

She was both mother and god. She was Wing Kong.

Of course, the government was called in, but still, Wing Kong and her bloodthirsty minions came by the million. Periodically, she would issue forth an ear-splitting sort of *shriek* to urge her oddly salmon-colored wingless progeny forward. She, too, had serrated teeth and could behead a fat cop in a blink, leaving his donut wobbling in midair. She sounded a bit like Gorgo, too. but she had a kind of early middle-aged Elsa Lanchester thing about her. I know.

On their way to the Rockies they converted all of life to hopeless dust. A limitless plain of dried dried shit remained, except for a few tired old farmers pissing on everything In sight. We were beaten.

We are stragglers on a stricken plain,
  sitting in a fog of chicken pain.
Redolent of canvas pants and rope-
  soled shoes,we are
In a pecked-clean flat and arid place.
  Wing Kong prowls
And pounds The Dakota lands from
  here to there.
She teeters across the flat and
  disappears, as today
The nuggets awake,
  From here to there, and Wing Kong
pounds around
  with nothing to do except to whack
a hopeless notch here and there,
  and then move on.

P.S. MUELLER is Staff Liar of *The American Bystander*.